'Holden helps us see the infant colony in a whole new way—through the vulnerable eyes of a child…an eloquent and imaginative writer who combines historical rigour with the popular appeal of a powerfully told tale.'
Age

'An important breakthrough in this neglected area of research into early transportation…First Fleeters will find this work essential reading as they expand their knowledge of a little researched subject.'
Canberra Times

'In this relatively short work of 180 pages, Holden has collated information from a commendably wide range of sources that both boggles the senses and stimulates the brain.'
Courier-Mail

'Holden makes an effort to color the ink of the available records with insights into family life in the early colony.'
Herald Sun

ALSO BY ROBERT HOLDEN
The Fairy World of Ida Rentoul Outhwaite
The Mechanical Eye and the Illustrated Book
Twinkle Twinkle Southern Cross: The Forgotten Folklore of Australian Nursery Rhymes
A Golden Age: Australian Fantasy Illustrators (2 vols)
Cover Up: The Art of Magazine Covers in Australia

ORPHANS OF HISTORY

THE FORGOTTEN CHILDREN
OF THE FIRST FLEET

ROBERT HOLDEN

TEXT PUBLISHING
MELBOURNE AUSTRALIA

Robert Holden is an art historian and authority on Australian children's literature. He lives in Sydney.

The Text Publishing Company
171 La Trobe Street
Melbourne Victoria 3000
Australia

First published 2000, reprinted 2000
This edition published 2000, reprinted 2001
Printed and bound by Griffin Press
Designed by Chong Weng-ho
Typeset in 11.3/15 Baskerville by J & M Typesetting

National Library of Australia
Cataloguing-in-Publication data:
Holden, Robert.
Orphans of history: the forgotten children of the First Fleet.
Bibliography.
ISBN 1 876485 54 X.
1. First Fleet, 1787–1788 - Biography. 2. Convicts - New
South Wales - Biography. 3. Children - New South Wales -
History - 1788–1851. 4. Children - New South Wales -
Social life and customs - 1788–1851. 5. Children - New
South Wales - Social conditions - 1788–1851. 6. Convicts -
Australia - History. I. Title.
994.402

This project has been assisted by the Commonwealth Government through the Australia Council, its arts funding and advisory body.

Australia Council
for the Arts

ILLUSTRATION SOURCES
p. 16 *Gin Lane*, William Hogarth, engraving and etching, 1751.
p. 37 frontispiece engraving in J. P. Andrews, *An Appeal to the Humane, on Behalf of…The Climbing Boys,* London, 1788. Courtesy British Library, London.
p. 39 handbill, 1787, from 18E reel, FM4/51 reel 6525, item 43. Courtesy Royal Society of Arts Library, London.
p. 65 *Interior of Newgate*, etching, c. 1785. Property of the author.
p. 75 and 80, engravings by William Jackson from *The New and Complete Newgate Calendar,* London, c. 1795. Courtesy British Library, London.
p. 130 *A Family of New South Wales*, sketch by Governor King, from John Hunter, *Journal of the Transaction at Port Jackson and Norfolk Island*, London, 1793.
p. 141 woodcut detail from a broadside, *A Description of a Wonderful Large Wild Man, or Monstrous Giant, Brought from Botany Bay*, c. 1790. Courtesy State Library of New South Wales.
p. 180 engraved headpiece from the *Punch Almanack*, May 1842.

FOR RICHARD

ACKNOWLEDGMENTS

This book has been as long and difficult a voyage for me as it was for the children I have written about. My greatest debt is to my family—to a wife and son whose love provided a lifeline which brought me through overwhelming seas, and to a twin brother who literally gave blood to keep me going.

In America, Ray Smith's hospitality and valued friendship gave me the opportunity to compare the *Mayflower*'s voyage with that of the First Fleet. They got the Pilgrims and we got the convicts—who was the luckiest?

Beyond these individual obligations I owe an inestimable debt to the specialists, nursing staff and volunteers of Sydney's St Vincent's Hospital and the Sacred Heart Hospice for a year of intensive care and their ongoing support thereafter.

Iain Hunter, Professor Phillip Jones (University of Sydney), Rosalind and Ian Hollinrake, David and Linda van Nunen, Diana Chicchio and Curtis Brown Literary Agents all offered succour along the way to Botany Bay.

The example and scholarship of Mollie Gillen's *Founders of Australia* inspired the very genesis of this work.

The patient staff in the Mitchell Library, State Library of New South Wales; the New South Wales Parliamentary Library; the Archives Office of New South Wales; the British Library (London) and the Public Records Office (Kew and Chancery Lane, London) are most sincerely acknowledged.

Marjorie Raven's staunch battle to secure Francis Hannah Clement a significant place on the First Fleet is to be congratulated. Janet O'Keffe, a descendant of the First Fleet family the Harmsworths, provided valuable genealogical information on their three children.

Michael Heyward's extreme patience and professionalism as a publisher and Melanie Ostell's sensitive editing are also gratefully acknowledged.

Finally, the author gratefully acknowledges the assistance of the Literature Board of the Australia Council whose writer's grant substantially underwrote research costs.

CONTENTS

'What—is—this?' he said at last.
'This is a child!…We only found it today. It's as large as life, and twice as natural!'
'I always thought they were fabulous monsters!' said the Unicorn. 'Is it alive?'

Lewis Carroll, *Through the Looking-Glass*

THE INFANT COLONY

> Going with child is as it were a rough sea, on
> which a big-belly'd woman and her infant floats
> the space of nine months: and labour, which is
> the only port, is so full of dangerous rocks, that
> very often both the one and the other, after they
> are arriv'd and disembark'd, have yet need of
> much help.
>
> Francois Mauriceau, 1668

CONCEPTION. Pregnancy. Birth.

An image of a mother and child, of a mewling infant attached
to the pendulous breasts of a gin-sodden mother. More Hogarth
than Gainsborough. Another image—one with all the crude exaggeration of the cartoon. Britain is the mother. The rapacious
infant is a convict colony halfway across the world in New
Holland.

This second image is no more than could be constructed from
the broadsides, political squibs, newspaper extracts, letters,
cartoons, graphic satires, fantasies and folklore of late eighteenth-
century Britain. It serves to take us away from any modern idea
of precious and protected childhood to something more pertinent
and truthful to our topic.

When the First Fleet sailed from Portsmouth on 13 May 1787
it consisted of eleven vessels. Scattered over six of these ships were
as many as thirty-four young voyagers under fourteen years of age.

After a protracted voyage of almost nine months this 'Noah's Ark of small-time criminality' added a further twenty children to its complement.[1] Allowing for three deaths, and six miscarriages and stillbirths, there were about fifty children present to witness the establishment of a convict settlement on the other side of the world. In 1788 the average age of these children was two and a half years old. These witnesses to a turning point in history have previously been overlooked, ignored or dismissed as of little consequence: they have remained invisible. It is time that Captain Arthur Phillip's forgotten children were woven back into history. It is time they were given a voice.

Why is it that any mention of these children in over two hundred years of official papers, log books, journals, musters and histories reduces them to mere footnotes? Their only presence has been as dumb witnesses to the most momentous historical event in white Australia's past. Why is it that we have not heard more of this singular group?

Most were 'free' children although close to half had one or both parents as convicts—the remainder were children of the marines. There may have been as many as twenty-seven children born on the voyage out with perhaps six failing to survive. The uncertainty of these numbers is due to unreliable records—Newgate Prison lists, journals, logs, victualling lists, embarkation lists, etc. are often incomplete and sometimes contradictory. Any list of children would hardly have been a priority in this situation which was so negligent of human documentation and so such records are arbitrary and rife with misspellings, approximations of names and omissions. To confound attempts at accuracy still further, Surgeon Bowes Smyth on board the *Lady Penrhyn* made two entirely different lists of its young passengers.

The eight-and-a-half-month voyage of the First Fleet may have been close to a full-term pregnancy, but one might well ask just what was delivered when the ships finally breached Sydney Heads in January 1788. The settlement itself was to be a new child of empire, separated from its parent by over 24,000 kilometres of ocean. And it was certainly a birth of sorts. It was a pregnant moment when thirty-seven mothers and their children stepped ashore in the infant colony in February 1788.

Largely hidden in a motley collection of 1500, these fifty children are now to be singled out as a significant group. The usual reaction of people on learning that there were children on the First Fleet is one of disbelief: 'What children? Surely the First Fleet was composed of the lowest men and women from the criminal classes who were exiled from their native land for its own good?' And while this particular and popular myth has been the focus of considerable historical questioning and revision, the claim that a substantial number of children landed at Sydney Cove in 1788 has seldom been raised before.

At this stage we must establish what it is that defines a British child in late eighteenth-century thinking.[2] Dr Johnson's great dictionary defined youth as 'fourteen years and above'. The standard legal reference work *Blackstone's Commentaries* is in agreement: 'Under 7 years of age…an infant cannot be guilty of felony…under 14…if it appears to the court and jury that he…could discern between good and evil, he may be convicted and suffer death.'[3] For our purposes, therefore, 'child' as opposed to 'youth' or 'juvenile' defines anyone up to the age of fourteen.

Of the thirty-four children who embarked on the First Fleet in 1787, two were elite young voyagers: a son and a nephew of officers aboard. Sixteen were the children of marines who had been permitted to bring their families with them. More surprisingly, there were three children who were themselves under convict sentence: Elizabeth Hayward, John Hudson and George Youngson. And what has been forgotten, overlooked or perhaps even dismissed as being of little consequence is that thirteen children accompanied their convict mothers. These thirteen ranged from a month-old boy to an eight-year-old girl.

The newborn child, William Tilley, had been delivered on the *Lady Penrhyn* before it sailed. Jane Jones, probably eight years old, also sailed on the *Lady Penrhyn*. Any surprise one feels in discovering that thirteen children accompanied their convict mothers into exile is, perhaps, overshadowed by the further realisation that their mothers had made a deliberate decision to take their offspring with them.

Petitions from two of these mothers to the Navy Board expressed their strong desire not to be separated from their children. Rebecca Bolton's mother was 'very desirous' to take her daughter with her.[4] The gaoler at Lincoln took a compassionate interest in her case and mother and daughter embarked together. Another more dramatic case was that of the infant Edward Parkinson and his mother Jane, who arrived at the *Dunkirk* hulk together in 1786: 'The Gaoler who delivered these people assured me, that every means, except force, were used in vain, to prevent the child being brought here, the mother declaring that she would destroy herself if separated from her Infant.'[5] The compassion of the authorities was forthcoming— the superintendent of the *Dunkirk* ended his letter with a plaintive request: 'Pray Sir inform me whether this little one is to accompany its mother to Botany Bay…'[6] Permission was granted although the mother was one of the few convicts who did not survive the long voyage. Her son Edward thus became the first child to be orphaned after the Fleet left England.

There were, as yet, no regulations regarding the conditions under which a child could accompany its convict mother to Botany Bay, and each case was considered on its merits. Once transportation to the Australian colonies became more regulated in the 1790s, other convict mothers were less fortunate than Bolton and Parkinson and the anguish of broken families howls through a 1791 report from the Philanthropic Society:

> An unhappy female in Newgate was sentenced to be transported to Botany-Bay for 14 years. Her husband was dead, and she had no friend in the world to take charge of two poor children, a little boy and girl, who were wandering desolate about the streets...Her great concern was for these unprotected children...Before she sailed for Botany-Bay, she was indulged with an interview with her children, proper officers being present; when few can conceive the violence of her emotions...[7]

Another female convict, when offered transportation for life to Botany Bay in lieu of the death penalty, refused 'on account of not being permitted to take her children with her, and was taken back to Newgate in strong convulsions, and her shrieks were re-echoed through the whole gaol'.[8]

The anguish of those convict mothers separated from their children is not found in the officers' journals and lavishly illustrated accounts of the First Fleet. Even the most passionate First Fleet diary, that of Lieutenant Ralph Clark, who continually laments his separation from his wife and young son, reveals little empathy with the fate of convicts' families. It is as if Clark and other officers believed finer feelings and deep emotions were solely the prerogative of the ruling class. By uncovering the determination of some convict mothers to take their children on the First Fleet we apprehend an emotional dimension that is absent from the accounts that survive.

There was, though, a form of publishing aimed at those who were less literate and who could only afford cheap and ephemeral publications. These were the broadsides, chapbooks, tracts, ballads and newspapers of the late eighteenth century. And while sentimental and romantic notions colour these popular accounts— the protagonists are presented as veritable folk heroes oppressed by the system—they do move us beyond eighteenth-century reticence and decorum into a new emotional dimension. One of these is a broadside, first published in the early nineteenth century, entitled *The Convict's Child*, which recounts in ballad form the separation of a convict father from his child:

> The convict ship lay near the beach,
> The morn was drear and dark,
> And many a wretched felon stood
> Awaiting to embark.
> One felon stood among the rest,
> His eye look'd fierce and wild!
> He held an infant in his arms
> 'Twas alas! his only child...
>
> They tore the infant from his arms,
> Then dragged him from the shore,
> He wildly gazed around the beach,
> But saw his child no more.
> The vessel sail'd—the convict fell—
> In dying anguish wild,
> 'Tis done, the fatal struggle's o'er,
> Alas, my only child.
>
> The widow sobbed alone,
> Her tears might flow in vain,
> That bitter morn her husband fell,
> She ne'er could see again.
> She pressed her infant to her breast,
> Again she saw him smile,

> 'I'll live for that dear boy,' she cried,
> 'Alas, my only child.'[9]

Broadsides like these were printed in their thousands for widespread distribution. Perhaps the most moving of all these ephemeral accounts is found in a tract published in 1796:

> The STORY of Poor TRICKET the Gamester Shewing How he first lost his place by gaming, and then had well nigh been the death of his wife through the same cause, and how last, his gaming was the occasion of his being transported as a convict to Botany Bay.

By the end of this piece the total destruction of a family unit by convict transportation is depicted:

> Tricket was convicted at the next assizes on the clearest evidence, and sentenced to death; but some favourable circumstances in his case were reported to his Majesty, by the Judge, and the sentence was in consequence changed from death to transportation.
>
> The fear of death at first made even Botany Bay appear a deliverance, but when he was to depart thither, bitter indeed, was the affliction of his faithful wife…She was earnestly desirous to go with him, but finding that she could not be allowed to take her children, she thought it her duty not to forsake them.[10]

The transportation of a convict was only one part of the punishment inflicted—there was also the effect their exile had on any dependants left behind. In the First Fleet, for example, the wife of the convict John Lockley reputedly died of distress after her husband's arrest; James Morrisby and John Owles each left behind a wife and five children; Richard Phillmore left three infants and two aged parents and Charlotte Ware left a fatherless child to the mercy of neighbours.

Such secondary economic and social effects of transportation failed to prompt any official inquiry into the distressed state of the families left behind, and we may never know the magnitude of the suffering. If, however, as a recent survey shows, about a quarter of the convicts transported to Australia together left almost 9000 children behind them, then an overall figure of many thousands more is certain.[11] Furthermore, the practical problems of family survival and destitute children seemed of little concern to benevolent agencies other than the Philanthropic Society:

> Most of our charitable institutions have confined their beneficence to the deserving, but unfortunate part of the community; whilst the offspring of the vicious and dishonest have been unhappily involved in the guilt of their parents...These unfortunate children are frequently forced on desperate courses; with blasted reputations, with dangerous connections, and coming from suspicious places...what private family will open a door to receive them?[12]

While it is true that these broken families could have applied to the parish for admission to the workhouse, this charity was only available to those who resided in the parish of their birth. Perhaps, under these circumstances, it was no worse for children to accompany their mothers to prison than it was to remain free and wandering the streets as destitute and vulnerable waifs? Perhaps it was no worse for their small presence to swell the numbers on the First Fleet?

Certainly the presence of children does not agree with our ideas and expectations as to the nature and structure of society in a penal colony. The British, and eventually the colonial authorities, recognised a need for the effective separation of juvenile and adult convicts during the long voyage to Australia, but it was not until thirty years after the First Fleet's arrival that boys were accommodated separately from the men convicts. The segregation of girls from women convicts was never considered at all. The policy of male segregation was most consistently observed in Van Diemen's Land where separate ships were later used as floating juvenile reformatories. And the eventual consignment of segregated boys to remote Point Puer in Tasmania ensured that their separate status was maintained.

For the sentenced children on the First Fleet, however, such considerations were as yet unthought of. Even so, one of Governor Phillip's first acts towards specific children in the colony shows that he did not regard the penal settlement as a fit place for the young. Within months of establishing the settlement he sent the Fleet's first orphan—Edward Parkinson, aged four or five—to Norfolk Island with six- or seven-year-old Mary Fowles, the daughter of a convict woman 'of abandoned character'.[13] This act of charity (or philanthropic abduction) was indicative of official attitudes which accepted that the children of convicts were better separated from their parents' dreadful influence and the geographical contamination of the settlement itself.

And, of course, it follows that if there were children on the First Fleet then there were also families. All too often interest in and emphasis on the First Fleet has been directed towards those who kept journals; the illustrious names who recorded our history in their shipboard diaries. Nevertheless, family units were not unusual on the Fleet, quite apart from the most obvious category consisting of the marines, their wives and children.

There was, for example, Lieutenant John Shortland and his two sons, who served as crew members: John jnr and his younger brother Thomas. There was the chaplain Richard Johnson and his wife Mary. There was the boatswain on the *Sirius* Thomas Brooks and his 'wife' Deborah, and at least one seaman and his wife: James and Martha Thring. Hidden in the musters was a pair of seafaring brothers, Thomas and Robert Webb, and at least two sets of convict brothers, Francis and Thomas MacLean and Daniel and Richard Smart. At least one married couple was transported as convicts, William and Ellen Fraser, and there was the convict pair of father and son, Noah and John Mortimer. These two successfully petitioned Governor Phillip in September 1788 to allow the remainder of their family to join them. Although this request was granted (in April 1789) because of their good behaviour, it is sad to find that their family did not follow them to Botany Bay and presumably they were never reunited. And, finally, there were at least two sets of convicts who were brothers and sisters: Thomas and Isabella Oldfield and George and Elizabeth Youngson.

This intimate breakdown of First Fleeters into their relationships serves as a sobering reminder of the manifold family units which were wrenched apart by convict transportation. It also reminds us that families were an integral part of the settlement from its very beginning. The most recent first volume of Alan Atkinson's *The Europeans in Australia*, which warrants comparison with Manning Clark's magnum opus for its sensitivity and magisterial scope, reinforces this perspective:

> New South Wales was the last of a little family of [British] settlements, the off-spring of empire in the age of enlightenment…Imaginative Englishmen now began to think in more elaborate terms [beyond public administration and mere survival of felons], to let their minds move among schemes which would bind families…to the soil on the other side of the sea, endowing them with a second birth and a new life, planning not for a voyage but for generations.[14]

If we are to trace this long voyage through the eyes of a child we need to single one out for particular attention. It would be remarkable to find someone who saw the whole founding enterprise through the eyes of a child and yet left a reliable record of his or her experiences. Unfortunately, it appears that no child kept a shipboard diary or sent letters home; most were illiterate or too young.

The only known exceptions to this could have been the two elite young voyagers Alexander John Ross and James Campbell. Both were possibly under ten years of age when they landed in the colony. They had travelled on the *Lady Penrhyn* and were drawn together as welcome company during the long voyage. Both were almost certainly educated enough for us to expect them to leave some record of their voyage. Surely either could have kept a diary or would at least have written to his mother left behind in England? The thought of finding such juvenile records is a heady draught for any researcher. In their absence we must reconstruct the shipboard life of children from adult sources which only occasionally and tantalisingly offer a glimpse of the life and experiences of the youngest members of the First Fleet.

So, which young First Fleeter should be our initial guide? Who should take us through late eighteenth-century London, through its feculent streets and horrific prisons to embarkation on the First Fleet and arrival in Sydney Cove? Could there have been anyone whose childhood encompassed such a range of experiences, someone who was young in years but old in crime?

Imagine for a moment—a London street urchin in 1783 and an Aboriginal boy in Sydney Cove in 1788. Could there have been any possible point of contact between the two? How could the worlds of Georgian England and New Holland have collided to effect a meeting of these apparent opposites?

Imagine still further the sooty imprints the hands and feet of a nine-year-old chimneysweep left on the wall of a London town-house in 1783 as he burgled its few treasures. Like his antipodean counterpart this boy was an adept climber and resourceful survivor. Perhaps their worlds were not opposites after all. Black with soot our white thief unknowingly left behind his 'signature'. Although otherwise certainly illiterate, his black prints were to be the damning evidence that the resourceful house owner copied and used at the Old Bailey to convict the hapless child.

Imagine the black print from this white boy alongside its exact antithesis—alongside the white stencil handprint of an Aboriginal boy half a world away. The inversions of nature, and of black for white, which the Antipodes offered are surely no more strongly portrayed than in these two images.

The real life saga of the London chimneysweep John Hudson, his crime and sentencing at nine, and his arrival in Australia on the First Fleet connected these two worlds. Once in Sydney Cove he became familiar with the sight of Aboriginal boys his own age who were free to visit the settlement. He may even have seen stencilled handprints the natives left on cliff faces and cave walls as their 'signature' of tribal initiation: a reminder of his own damning prints back in London.

Such a confrontation might seem little short of melodrama, but then history is never far removed from histrionics. Such a meeting of cultures and joining of hands, however, has real resonance. It moves our story beyond a set piece on the grand stage of late eighteenth-century history to a more intimate and human level. It reminds us that the imprints of history are often created by the forgotten, and that history is as much about the joining of hands across time as it is about the broken links between generations.

John Hudson, chimneysweep and petty criminal, had a place in the infant settlement amongst a range of over 700 convicts. They included the near-aristocratic and the unlettered; the juvenile offender perhaps as young as thirteen and the aged felon of sixty-eight. He was among English, Irish, Scottish, Welsh, French, North

American and black convicts. The Fleet was loaded down with provisions which included millions of nails, thousands of squares of glass, 8000 fish hooks and, a touch of unexpected refinement, a pianoforte. Among this diverse assemblage there is perhaps nothing that could raise our sympathies or our surprise more than to discover the presence of these children. How much more remarkable then, in the light of this extraordinary range of provisions, to find that no real allowance or forethought was made for these children at all.

Today, historical interpretation has advanced as one of its main goals the breaking down of a them-and-us mentality with regard to the convicts. It is strange that their humanity, their links with us have become clearer rather than more obscured with the passing of time. And how distant is 1788 anyway? Sarah Nicolls, a child of a First Fleeter died in 1907.

One of the most popular novels of the eighteenth century, at least talked about if not read by a vast cross-section of the population, was Daniel Defoe's *Moll Flanders*, published in 1722. The adventures and vicissitudes of its chameleon-like heroine are succinctly stated in the subtitle: 'Twelve Years a Whore, Five times a Wife...Twelve Years a Thief, Eight Years transported Felon...at last...lived Honest, and died a Penitent.' Today we are prepared to see that Moll's protean lifestyle was replicated in Botany Bay. Rather than view the female convicts as unregenerate whores, the male convicts as the most degenerate criminals and the whole batch as the illiterate refuse of society, historical revisionism casts them as foundation mothers, entrepreneurial pioneers and semi-literate victims.

But where are the children in this new historical inquiry? And why should we single out this small group for historical scrutiny?

The reasons are varied, but this focus enables us to question further assumptions and preconceptions about these early years. We realise that family life did exist under these adverse conditions, that there were stable family relationships at all levels of colonial society and that everyone, children included, adapted to colonial conditions. Most significantly, we learn that these children were not part of a homogeneous group and that no single experience defines their various lives. On the most obvious level they formed a link between the two divisions of society, the free and the convicted. The peculiar structure of colonial life was not abnormal for many of these children. Most of them were not tied down by the past experience of a British life. By singling out this group we could attempt to trace the impact of the colonial experience on these unfettered souls.

Even if all the answers are not forthcoming, the most important thing is that at last these questions are being raised. The children of the First Fleet are being born again into historical recognition and inquiry. At last these orphans of history are being given back their place in our past.

LONDON 1783

> Idle and disorderly persons of both sexes and of
> all descriptions are everywhere to be met with,
> many of them in a state of perpetual vagrancy,
> profligate, discarded and miserable in the
> extreme, a nuisance and expense to the commu-
> nity and a standing reproach to the government
> under which they live.

H. Zouch, 1786

LONDON, late in the year 1783. Paradise to some, hell to others. The scene of Canaletto's majestic and measured townscapes and Hogarth's sink of sin. Images painted by these artists some years earlier still provide a succinct dichotomy of what the metropolis offered towards the end of the eighteenth century .

In 1783 the Thames served as both the chief source of domestic water and the main outlet for personal and commercial waste. Human ordure piled up around houses in stinking cesspools. These cesspools often overflowed, were infrequently emptied, and sometimes leaked into wells and cellars. Excreta was also dumped into street drains and open sewers. Without running water those channels stagnated and festered.

The outcome was predictable. London repeatedly fell victim to fever epidemics, especially bouts of dysentery and typhus. In such feculent conditions perhaps no-one was more at home than the London chimneysweep. He is the one figure of the time

William Hogarth, *Gin Lane*, 1751. Hogarth's urban mayhem depicts a violent and licentious society, including an infant falling to its death after suckling from its drunken mother.

who broached the two worlds of Hogarth and Canaletto; who managed the transition from the deepest pit of squalor to the grandest homes in the land.

And a London chimneysweep is our guide through this late eighteenth-century world of contrasts. A guide whose cloacal journeys through the secret intestines of houses led him straight to Newgate Prison and to an antipodean penal colony. John Hudson could have counted the celebrated English highwayman John Cottington (1611–56) among his predecessors. Another who made a 'natural' progression from young chimneysweep to criminal, Cottington had been apprenticed to a mastersweep at the age of eight, ran away at thirteen and, after a long life of crime, died on the gallows.

Although John Hudson was hardly a celebrated outlaw, he was a noteworthy figure among the convicts who embarked on the First Fleet in 1787. His extreme youth alone was enough to differentiate him from the mass of his fellow convicts on board. And his presence can lead us to uncover the fifty children who made a sizeable, albeit forgotten, contribution to the Fleet's company.

So, again, London. Specifically, October 1783. And more specifically, East Smithfield, an area of 'flash houses' or inns which were popular meeting places for criminal gangs. This was not the London of great streets and squares, of pleasure gardens like Ranelagh and Vauxhall, of the wealthy shopping precincts of Pall Mall and The Strand. This London was a warren of lanes, alleys, courts and by-places in which, according to Henry Fielding, 'the whole appears as a vast wood or Forest, in which a Thief may harbour with as great security, as wild Beasts do in the Deserts of Africa or Arabia'.[1] Another novelist, Tobias Smollett, saw a similar London in the 1770s: 'An immense wilderness in which there is neither watch nor word of any signification, nor any order of police, [which] affords…[criminals] lurking-places as well as prey.'[2]

At one o'clock in the morning, as dark as the hour and the pall from coal fires made it, with only main thoroughfares illuminated by oil lamps and many streets an obstacle course of open sewers, uneven stones and refuse, there was still traffic about. The patrolling of the streets by the precursors of a police force was a rudimentary exercise by frequently infirm old men. They bore no arms other than a stout pole and carried a lanthorn to light their way as well as a wooden rattle to summon help. They were easily bribed and it was common for them to be beaten for sport by drunken gangs. In short, London at one o'clock in the morning was conducive to criminal activity.

Throughout the eighteenth century law enforcers and the general public grew apprehensive about the escalating crime rate. In 1701 an anonymous pamphlet entitled 'Hanging Not Punishment Enough' was published, and in 1796 *A Treatise on the Police of the Metropolis* appeared. Nearly a hundred years separated these two documents of warning, yet crime in England was rampant and London had become a city under siege. No man's house was safe unless it was fortified by palisades and redoubts and defended by a small army of servants. Even the king was not safe—George III was robbed of his watch, money and shoe buckles while walking in the gardens of Kensington Palace one evening.

At one o'clock in the morning on this early London day it was almost time for the watch to cry the hour. Two young boys sidled down the street, seemingly oblivious to the filth and manure they walked through in bare feet. After the evening's events one of the boys would enter the pages of Australian convict history: John Hudson was to become the youngest convict of the First Fleet in 1787.

Hudson's event-filled story of juvenile destitution and criminal temptation could have been turned into a moralising tract or chapbook. A range of readers from children and the semi-literate to the more sophisticated would have accepted Hudson's adventures as popular, suitable and credible reading. And if his story had reached publication, it would have been its cautionary nature as much as its narration of perilous adventures that would have popularised it.

Such ephemeral publications were yet another version of the stern finger of authority from church and state admonishing all to exemplary lives. One such work published in John Hudson's own day about Little Jem the chimneysweep assembled all these attributes into a moving and, possibly, real-life account.

Ultimately, John and Little Jem are interchangeable. Beyond the similarity of their names and the occupation they had in common, both were orphans. Two young boys cast out on the streets of eighteenth-century London without family or guardians; without any friend or any agency of care to oversee their future.

Little Jem's harrowing twenty-page tale is a litany of cruel exploitation. Its publication is evidence of the public's increasing concern for unfortunate street children and particularly chimneysweeps. In the absence of any information on John Hudson's life before his crime in 1783, Jem's sorry tale is probably as close as we will ever get to a vision of Hudson's own early days: 'When I was five years old...master wanted an apprentice, and so I was sent to him...I work hard, have little to eat, and often get drubbed into the bargain.'[3]

Little Jem (Little John) was consigned to a desperate and hopeless future:

> He had the misfortune to be bound apprentice to a
> brutal master...one of these abandoned characters,
> who fear neither God nor devil. With regard to the
> boys in his power, his only care was not to injure them
> so much as to make himself punishable by the laws of

the land, and if he avoided that he thought himself at
liberty to treat them as ill as he chose. When he was
in his passions therefore he would thrash them in a
most unmerciful manner, lock them up without food
till they were ready to faint, or turn them out of doors
on the coldest nights in winter.[4]

In short, apprentices such as these young boys were utter
outcasts. Their labours confined them to a sooty wasteland by day
which turned them into 'young Africans of our own growth'—that
is, into home-grown slaves.[5]

For any mastersweep to set up in business the initial capital
investment was minimal—some rope, a ladder, brushes and scrap-
ers, bags for carrying soot and, of course, one small boy. The
mastersweep did not need to pay anything for a boy from the
almshouse, a common and popular source for such labour. In fact,
he might have even received a small premium for his 'favour' to
cover the fee of the indenture papers. Although young boys
like Little Jem were sought after as apprentice chimneysweeps,
their market value was negligible. Destitute and orphan children
with no government agency to look out for their welfare were easy
prey to such masters. And, since the boys traditionally begged for
food as well as for the rags to clothe themselves, their living
expenses were nonexistent.

It is in this context of utter desperation that Little Jem's master
intimidates him. He attempts to persuade Jem to steal plate from a
house he is engaged to enter and sweep. When these arguments fail,
Little Jem is threatened with a beating in an attempt to gain his
reluctant co-operation. But the boy is adamant. Unlike John Hudson,
who actively pursued criminal activities, Little Jem fulfils a literary
and evangelical purpose and steadfastly remains an innocent.

Jem's refusal to steal prompts his master to undertake the
task himself. When the crime is discovered the real thief hides

incriminating evidence on Little Jem and it is the boy who is gaoled. At the penultimate moment, in true melodramatic fashion, the only thing that saves the sweep is a death-bed confession from his master.

Were John Hudson's story not inscribed in legal records as a real-life saga, we could imagine that it belonged to this genre of popular fiction. But John is not a literary construction. He was a willing, even initiating agent in his own downfall. We cannot romanticise his story and turn it into an act of bravado, of young impetuosity or even of coercion.

On that dark London night of October 1783, John Hudson was nine years old. There is evidence that he was already skilled in a life of risk-taking and of self-sufficiency, if not in the world of petty crime. With an accomplice he broke a narrow skylight above a window in the house they targeted. The glass was 'taken perfectly out' which suggests that the two were accomplished housebreakers.[6] They then proceeded to steal 'one linen shirt, value 10s., five silk stockings, value 5s., one pistol, value 5s., and two aprons, value 2s.'.[7] It was John Hudson's sooty imprints that gave him away. His marks on a table near the broken skylight inspired the enterprising householder to take their impression on a sheet of paper. This evidence clearly pointed towards the culprit being a child, and a chimneysweep.

A few days after the burglary, Hudson was seen nearby trying to wash his soot off at a water tub. It appeared he had secreted his loot in the vicinity and returned to the scene of the crime to retrieve it. He was arrested as soon as his cache was uncovered. Within three days, according to the regulations, he was examined before a justice, and two months later appeared at the Old Bailey. (This was the popular name for the Justice Hall adjoining Newgate Prison and it was there that almost half of all the convicts on the First Fleet were indicted.) After an extremely brief hearing

Hudson escaped a death sentence and was instead sentenced to seven years' transportation 'to some of His Majesty's Colonies & Plantations in America'.[8]

Such a sentence was to be the standard fate for most First Fleet convicts, although in December 1783 the actual place convicts were to be sent was in some doubt. America had just won its independence. Would it still accept convicts as before? Beyond this uncertainty John Hudson also had to face the gross inconsistencies in the penal system that were glaringly revealed in the treatment and transportation of children. It should not be forgotten that these young offenders could have been executed—as late as 1831 a nine-year-old boy was publicly hanged for arson. Only children under the age of seven were safe, although this exemption was generally extended up to the age of fourteen. At least six children aged between nine and twelve at their time of sentencing were sent on the Second Fleet in 1789: Samuel Cooley, William Butts, James Whitehouse, Mary Wade, Peter Buckeridge and Thomas Hemmings. Later still, in 1837, five children between eight and eleven were sentenced to up to ten years' transportation.[9] It is clear that mere youth was not a disqualification for transportation.

The details of John Hudson's crime and trial provide a sobering picture of a typical young offender's life and condition in the 1780s. Although Hudson's plaintive voice was only briefly heard in the court records we can reconstruct something of his experience as he faced the judge and jury in the Old Bailey—an experience that must have been intimidating, confusing and somewhat unintelligible.

On the day of his trial Hudson, along with other prisoners, was herded into the Old Bailey's open yard, surrounded on three sides by a high spiked wall. It was mid-December and, in spite of the weather, he and his companions were kept waiting at the court's pleasure. Earlier in the century these trials were mostly open-air affairs and must have resembled nothing so much as a great Punch and Judy show. And even when the court was enclosed (from 1737) the proceedings still operated as a form of popular entertainment and spectacle.

At John Hudson's trial, what may have been considered a touch of eighteenth-century refinement—the judge and jury holding nosegays of fresh herbs—was really an attempt to counter the stench of the prisoner in the dock. It was also a device to prevent the spread of 'gaol fever', otherwise known as typhus. One authoritative report of 1784 even declared that, from the 1750s until 1771, the annual average of executions in London was less than the annual average of prisoners who died from gaol fever.[10]

The prisoners were taken to the court from Newgate through a connecting passage. For what small consolation it was, Hudson and his fellow-prisoners no longer had to enter the Old Bailey via the street and through crowds of curious spectators. When Hudson's time came his indictment was read out. His was a crime against property—against the very basis on which the law was founded—and he was charged with 'burglariously and feloniously breaking and entering...and feloniously stealing'.[11] According to one modern historian this was 'the most commonly encountered capital crime of the eighteenth century' and to some it seemed that the country was almost under siege by thieves and housebreakers.[12] In his political pamphlet 'Hints Respecting the Public Police', H. Zouch wrote:

> It is a malancholy [sic] truth, that in every part of the kingdom (in the Metropolis, more particularly,) robbery is actually become a science; crimes of the deepest and most atrocious dye, are perpetuated in so open and daring a manner, and every species of fraud and deceit, is carried on with such wicked ingenuity, and address, as to baffle the utmost efforts of the ablest men to check the progress of them.[13]

A succinct recitation of the charge against John Hudson was then read. It included a valuation of the stolen goods to a total of twenty-two shillings. There followed a brief exchange of four questions and answers between the judge and the prisoner. John Hudson's responses—a mere thirteen words—convey the suffering of poor and abandoned children in London at the time with a force which spans the intervening centuries:

> Court to Prisoner: 'How old are you?'
> 'Going on nine.'
> 'What business was you bred up in?'
> 'None, sometimes a chimney sweeper.'
> 'Have you any father or mother?'
> 'Dead.'
> 'How long ago?'
> 'I do not know.'[14]

This is all the child said to the court. In line with the practice of the day he was not represented by counsel. Such assistance was only possible if a point of law arose, which prompts the question: what kind of defence could be prepared when the prisoners were denied access to depositions and to the names of witnesses against them? How much more difficult would it have been for, presumably, an uneducated and illiterate young prisoner like John Hudson to summon the confidence to face the court with some fortitude, let alone find the words to plead his case? He had no defence to offer. Could he have grasped the enormity of his situation?

Perhaps our modern sentiments should not be too readily aroused at the thought of this nine year old facing the court. The runners who arrested him told one witness it was 'the third time they had had him within ten days'.[15] Whether he was an experienced malefactor or not, Hudson's two months in prison before his court appearance certainly would have added to his criminal education. Without any segregation from adult offenders, his days and nights would have been full of the mock-heroics of those awaiting trial, of stories of bravado and cunning. He was a child imprisoned in a nursery of vice.

A number of things about the pace and quality of the trial mark it as radically different from any twentieth-century court experience: the hearing was scheduled only a short time after the crime's occurrence; and it was conducted in a conversationally informal mode, with the judge freely using his power to comment on the merits of the case. The speed of trials and rapid processing of the cases, quite usual for the day, must have thrown Hudson and similar prisoners into some confusion, and may have caused them to doubt that they were receiving a fair and patient hearing.[16]

John Hudson did not speak in his own defence, and there was no-one to speak for him. He was a nine-year-old child alone in his misery, fears and confusion. Were there any character witnesses? Surely there must have been one particular person who could have come forward on his behalf? Wasn't it conceivable that the master-sweep to whom John was apprenticed might have appeared and offered some support for the young offender? Did the world at large even know, or care, about this lonely ordeal?

And yet Hudson was not entirely without support and assistance. He did not face an impersonal and one-sided trial. Because the child was without counsel, the judge had to bear the responsibility for seeing that the proceedings were sufficient in law. And it is clear that this particular judge was concerned, if not solicitous, for the child. Judicial reservations resound throughout the court record:

> I wanted to see whether he had any understanding or no...I do not much like the confession of a boy of nine years old, I would rather do without it if I

could...That is threatening him, I cannot take a boy's
confession after that...Did the boy seem to want
understanding before the Justice?...Did he appear to
you to want understanding?[17]

'Understanding.' Three times this word rings out in the judge's
address. This judicial concern came from centuries of British legal
precedent which had established the principle: 'The capacity of
doing ill, or contracting guilt, is not so much measured by years
and days, as by the strength of the delinquent's understanding and
judgement.'[18] Up to the age of seven, in John Hudson's day, it was
presumed that children were incapable of criminal intent and
could not be held responsible for violations of the law, though a
death sentence was possible for a child under fourteen.

Between the ages of seven and fourteen children were
presumed innocent unless the prosecution proved their ability to
discern between good and evil. Once children reached fourteen
they had attained the age of discretion. Even so, age by itself gave
no right to special treatment and children were tried with the full
publicity and formality of the courts. Children were sentenced to
the same retributive punishments as adults. Fortunately, there were
individual magistrates and judges who could and did exercise
compassionate discretion. In John Hudson's case the judge
displayed benevolence and responded with care after scrutiny of
the case's merits. In his closing address to the jury he declared, 'I
do not think [Hudson's confession] should be allowed because it
was made under fear; I think it would be too hard to find a boy of
his tender age guilty of the burglary.'[19]

And so the child was declared not guilty of the burglary charge,
but guilty of breaking and entering. The judge obviously considered youth to be a strong mitigating circumstance. This attitude
is also clearly linked to a belief in the potential reform of the young
offender and to the hope that once removed from pernicious

connections he stood a better chance of that reform. The court seemed to consider that transportation was a kindness in that it removed Hudson from the corrupting influence of adult criminals:

> One would wish to snatch such a boy, if one possibly could, from destruction, for he will only return to the same kind of life which he has led before, and will be an instrument in the hands of very bad people, who make use of boys of that sort to rob houses.[20]

While the court appeared to accept that Hudson had an accomplice, there was no suggestion or pressure that this person testify against his companion in crime. In line with the standard legal practice of the day such a testimony may have secured Hudson's release. We have seen how the legal system depended on stimulating private enterprise, on citizens themselves gathering evidence for their case. Equally, the judiciary depended on encouragements to criminals to betray their accomplices. John presumably knew nothing of this. At any rate, he had confessed his crime even if the judge's closing remarks express some doubts as to its validity.

The judge's constant advocacy of the prisoner's cause—he even seemed at times to argue against the evidence—spared Hudson from a possible death sentence, which a charge of burglary could have attracted. A prison sentence was not an option. Eighteenth-century justice regarded prison as a place of transit, not as an ultimate destination and, except for debtors, most offenders faced punishment rather than incarceration.

The idea of prison as a reformatory was not yet popular, and the idea of prison as a punishment would have seemed an absurd expense. Even so, for those sentenced to transportation there could be a long wait in gaol and on the hulks before they were transported. Hudson, sentenced in December 1783, did not embark for the Antipodes until 1787.

CHIMNEYSWEEP TO CONVICT

ONE final aspect of John Hudson's early life, as revealed in the court records, invites and repays closer scrutiny. This is his description of himself as 'sometimes a chimney sweeper'.

We may think this is picturesque, perhaps even quaint, yet an examination of the harsh reality of a chimneysweep's life dispels any such sentiments. Early in the eighteenth century a practice seemingly peculiar to England arose which transformed small boys (and sometimes even small girls) into human brushes. It was accepted that flues would be better cleaned this way than by men with long birch brooms, or weighted ropes with a bunch of twigs tied to the centre.

Although various industrial and philanthropic societies offered premiums for a mechanical device to supersede such child labour, even when one was invented early in the nineteenth century the public continued to approve the use of children. The appalling result was documented by a horrified Samuel Roberts in 1824:

> [Chimneysweeps] are exposed to the unrestrained
> capricious cruelty of one of the most ignorant,
> violent, depraved classes of human beings in this or
> perhaps any other civilized kingdom...They have
> been precipitated from the tops of high
> chimnies...and dashed upon the pavement below.
> They have been slowly roasted to death in the flue of
> an oven. They have been dug dead out of the sides of
> chimnies, in which they have been stuck fast...[1]

This was the vicious world our young criminal inhabited. And, most significantly, we should not miss the telltale 'sometimes' in his statement which reveals the intermittent nature of his occupation. Could life have been any more difficult for little John? A nine-year-old orphan on the streets, who 'sometimes' worked, with hours spent in similar company. A life of crime seemed inevitable, and it was his 'sometimes' occupation, his climbing skills, which delivered him into the hands of the law. Once boys like John Hudson became too big to navigate the narrow flues they were cast aside with no other trade to secure them a living. Many fell foul of the law because their climbing skills provided an easy apprenticeship to burglary. And so it was for John.

Older chimneysweeps, also guilty of housebreaking and burglary, accompanied Hudson into convict exile: James Baldwin, about thirty, and Thomas Till, about twenty, were both sentenced to death in 1785, which was later commuted to seven years' transportation on the First Fleet. Presumably, because of their age, these two no longer worked as sweeps and fell into a life of urban crime. Having outgrown their 'profession' they were 'turned out upon the world with emaciated constitutions, with injured frames, without education, without information, without any means of supporting themselves...[with] no subsistence or employment...they must have recourse to robbery and plunder.'[2] One cannot help wondering if Baldwin and Till ever fraternised with the young John Hudson at sea; if they exchanged stories of their days as chimneysweeps and of their exploits as burglars.

A witness in John Hudson's case at the Old Bailey in 1783 gave evidence that on the morning after the robbery she saw the boy in a yard near the burgled house. 'He was going to wash himself; he was all sooty.'[3] The sight of a chimneysweep troubling to wash himself was a rare occurrence and aroused the witness' utmost suspicions. A claim before a parliamentary committee in 1788 on the habits of chimneysweeps stated there were 'many Instances of Boys who have served Four or Five Years without being at all washed'.[4] It was believed that if boys were washed every day their skin would be kept so tender they would be unable to perform their hard work. To the sweeps, washing was another form of punishment! Little wonder that the sight of a chimneysweep voluntarily washing himself at a drinking tub aroused interest and suspicion.

After that encounter events moved quickly. Others were called into the yard. A cache of clothes and a pistol were found. Hudson was apprehended. His quick denial was followed by a confession—after his sooty imprint 'was measured by the paper he then confessed he had been in the house'.[5] However inept the police, however much the collecting of evidence was the householder's initiative, however much John Hudson owed to sheer bad luck, he was now marked for prison and, even possibly, for hanging.

Most of us are familiar with Dickens' *Oliver Twist* and Kingsley's *The Water Babies*. As daunting as the depiction of exploitation and child labour may be in these novels, they do not convey the full horror of the young chimneysweep's experience. All child labour was damaging to the physique and morals of the young and, when coupled with romantic notions about childhood, this labour became an offence against innocence itself. But in 1783 such opinions and attitudes were not yet popular, although that very year marked the beginning of a campaign to alert the public to the plight of the chimneysweep.

According to modern historian Dorothy George, before the 1780s it was widely felt that chimneysweeps were 'villains ripening for the gallows rather than...objects of compassion'.[6] A shift in opinion can be dated from 1783, when the philanthropist Jonas Hanway published the first of three works on chimneysweeps. Hanway (1712–86) helped merge private charitable activity with public policy, and the steadfast concern he showed for the particular plight of sweeps inaugurated a growing public awareness of and debate about their dreadful situation.

There was to be more than a full century of desperation and suffering, though, before Hanway's concern was finally vindicated through Lord Shaftesbury's parliamentary victory which abolished the trade in 1875. Lord Shaftesbury had been appointed parliamentary adviser on child welfare in 1832 and his first bill to parliament on the deplorable condition of chimneysweeps was presented in 1851. Although 1875 marks his final victory with this cause it also, sad to say, marks the last year in which the death of a young chimneysweep on the job was reported: eleven-year-old George Brewster.[7] The death of this child and the subsequent trial and sentencing of a master chimneysweep were widely publicised in the British press. *The Times*, in particular, thundered out in righteous indignation. The nation was abashed.

While we can visualise in detail the late eighteenth-century world which John Hudson inhabited, is it possible to form an honest image of the child himself, or is he merely a disembodied voice briefly heard in his court appearance? We can certainly see him as a grimy and underfed street urchin whose labour may have left him with misshapen legs if not an actual limp. In 1785, Hanway reported that chimneysweeps were 'generally bandy-leg'd. Beginning to climb before the bone has acquired a solidity, the daily pressure necessarily gives the leg a twist, if it does not distort the ancles.'[8] They were also prone to a deformity of the spine from 'being obliged to ascend chimneys at an age when their bones are in a soft and growing state; but likewise, by their being compelled to carry bags of soot and cloths, the weight of which sometimes exceeds 20 or 30 pounds'.[9]

Although no image exists of the orphaned John Hudson, nor has any physical description of him been found in legal documents, we can surmise something of his appearance by knowing he was a sweep. He was a child of the streets, undernourished and small. A survivor. His neglected and abandoned status made him a prime candidate for mastersweeps to exploit. Their boys were 'generally taken from the illegitimate children of the lowest kind of people, from the vagabond orphans who wander about the streets'.[10] This description from James P. Andrews in 1788 certainly fits John Hudson and his daily companions.

Visualise little John then. Jonas Hanway, his most assiduous advocate, wrote:

> We seldom behold [the chimneysweep's] nocturnal toils…but in the day we frequently see him, blasted with chilling cold, wet to the skin, without shoes, or with only the fragments of them; without stockings; his coat and breeches in tatters, and his shirt in smutty rags; sometimes with sores bleeding, or with limbs twisted or contracted.[11]

A sympathetic mastersweep in 1788 provided a little more detail:

> If we would see this poor apprentice as he really is, let us view him in a wintry morning, exposed to the surly blast or falling snow, trudging the streets half naked, his sores bleeding, his limbs contracted with cold, his

inhuman master driving him beyond his strength,
whilst the piteous tears of hunger and misery trickle
down his cheek…follow him home, and view him in
his gloomy cell…in a cellar, used as a soot warehouse
on one side, and his lodging room on the other.'[12]

Understandably, mastersweepers favoured undersized boys,
who would be turned into little black slaves—veritable human
brushes. 'Little boys for small flues' was a popular phrase printed
on the business cards and handbills which mastersweepers left at
the doors of potential customers.

Chimneysweeps like John Hudson were recruited from as
young as four years of age. The industry needed small boys whose
bones were still malleable enough to negotiate chimney flues which
could be as small as 9 x 14 inches (23 x 35 centimetres).
Sometimes, Andrews wrote, these boys were 'driven up chimneys
by dints of menaces, nay by actual scorching…when such
chimnies have been so very narrow as to tear the skin and flesh
from the backs of the helpless sufferer'.[13] The 'menaces' used to
overcome the terror of the pitch-black and suffocating chimneys
were appalling: 'the more humane masters would threaten to beat
them, or perhaps only promise them plum pudding at the top; the
less humane would set straw on fire below or thrust pins into their
feet.'[14] New recruits were even confined for hours in the flues to
accustom them to the harsh conditions.

The sweeps were employed to scrape the soot from the sides of
the flue, replace the mortar which had become dislodged and
repair cracks in the brickwork. Oven chimneys were particularly
unpleasant as deposits of congealed fat and soot made it difficult
to get any firm grip. Constant lacerations were a permanent part
of life. For some a relatively quick death by asphyxiation or by
smoke inhalation may have been preferable to the long-term
sufferings which were an occupational hazard and which might

have included asthma, inflammation of the eyes, burned limbs, malformed spines and legs and tuberculosis. Most horrifyingly, these young children often developed cancer of the scrotum. According to Andrews:

> A cancerous disorder frequently attacks the most tender and delicate parts. This being generally unheeded at first, and its malignant properties being nourished by the heating quality of the soot, aided by the perpetual state of unwashed dirt and filthiness in which these wretched children are kept, at length increases to a degree which requires the care of an hospital; nor then can the cure be often effected without such operations (nay amputations) as render the unfortunate lads complete eunuchs.[15]

When Hanway's *A Sentimental History of Chimney-Sweepers* was published in 1785 the sentiments expressed were so novel that a new language was embraced to express its concern. Children were now 'an heritage, and a gift which come of the Lord...given...to increase the prosperity of a nation'.[16] Furthermore, childhood was now beginning to be viewed as a unique and blessed state of innocence that should be treasured and protected at all levels of society:

> In a well-regulated free community, every child is as much an object of the protection of the state as the adult...If these children are the offspring of the poorest people, the greater their poverty, the stronger their claim to protection in common rights.[17]

Hanway's conclusion was damning: 'There are many other occupations which shorten life, but none in which the helpless infant, in his sacred state of life, is so much violated.'[18] A great part of the novelty of these statements lies in the fact that they describe children of working age rather than earlier and younger philanthropic targets like foundlings.

The most profitable and dangerous part of the sweep's business was to extinguish chimneys which were still burning. For this task the boys entered the mouth of the chimney carrying a candle in their teeth and a scraper in their hands. They climbed by way of their knees and elbows to the top and then worked their way down. The 1788 parliamentary committee must have listened with horror to the story of a ten-year-old boy who was:

> sent up a chimney which had been on Fire for 48 Hours…during the Time he was up the Chimney, his Master came, and found fault with him, in so angry a Manner, as to occasion a Fright by which Means he fell down into the Fire, and was much burnt, and crippled by it for life.[19]

So greatly did boys fear chimney-sweeping that it is not strange to read of one who in 1819 consented to the amputation of a leg which had been crushed in a fall. When the surgeon assured the child that he would never again ascend a chimney with only one leg, *The Times* reported that he gladly accepted his fate.[20]

We can therefore imagine John Hudson, bleary-eyed from soot and knapped-kneed from climbing, by looking at the 1788 frontispiece to J. P. Andrews' *An Appeal to the Humane, on behalf of the most Deplorable Class of Society, The Climbing Boys, employed by the chimney-sweepers*. Hudson could have been one of the two young boys dwarfed by the imposing dome of St Paul's, a street child brought stage-centre in front of one of London's proudest monuments. It is an indictment on the city itself.

Although the number of sweeps was small they were the most visible of all the child labourers—they were not incarcerated in factories or mines away from the public eye but were a familiar sight in London and other major cities. Chimneysweeps like John

The abject child of Misery's sad train
Still looks on one below

Frontispiece to J. P. Andrews' work on chimneysweeps in 1788. The ragged misshapen boys in the foreground are dwarfed by the grandeur of St Paul's Cathedral, which further emphasises their piteous state.

Hudson were engaged in 'calling the streets' from the dark hours before dawn until midday. Thereafter they were free to roam the city in company with vagrants and beggars, plot their pathetic crimes and generally be considered as making up 'the greatest nursery for Tyburn of any trade in England'.[21]

Perhaps because of their sooty faces, their 'sable hue' as well as their subhuman condition, it was inevitable that the language of the slave trade was appropriated to the cause of sweeps. Samuel Roberts' poem 'The Chimney-Sweepers' Boy' clearly illustrates the tyranny the boys were subject to:

> Poor wretched sufferer! is this freedom's shore?
> Are there no slaves in England? Never more
> Let Britain boast that hers is freedom's land,
> While foot of infant slave pollutes her strand.
> The innocent, the helpless, native poor
> Are bought and sold, e'en at our very door!
> Are scourged, are wounded, crippled, maim'd, and driven
> To tasks more horrid than were ever given
> To other slaves! to climb where brutes would die,
> Through smothering soot, to rocking turrets high;
> Through rugged flues, that tear the tender frame,
> Through death's most hideous portal, scorching flame;
> To hang, close wedged, immoveable, where none
> Can aid impart till life itself is gone;
> Or waste away, with festering sore on sore,
> Till outraged nature can support no more!
> And are there slaves like these? There are! But where?
> In every street their piercing cry we hear,
> Yet heed it not—because 'twas always there.[22]

If we look beyond the camouflage that rhyme and rhythm give to the verse we see the little black slave that John Hudson was in

Richard Branſon,

Chimney-Sweeper & Nightman,

(LIVING at No. 394,)

Oppoſite CECIL-STREET,

Near the ADELPHI in the STRAND;

PERFORMS the Chimney-Sweeping Buſineſs in all its Branches; Extinguiſhes Chimneys when on Fire, with the greateſt care and ſafety; cleans Smoak-Jacks, and cures Smoaky Coppers, having clean Cloths, and always attends with the Boys himſelf, and will always be obliged to any Perſon that pleaſe to employ me.

Any Perſon that pleaſes to ſend to my House, ſhall be immediately waited on, by Day or Night.

☞ Pleaſe to take care of this Bill to prevent Miſtakes.

Handbill of a mastersweeper advertising his trade, 1787.

1783: as a chimneysweep he was more of a slave then than he was as a convict in Australia in 1788.

When the British parliament abolished Negro slavery in 1808, the chimneys of its august chambers were still being climbed by boys as young as four, who were sold by their parents to master-sweeps or apprenticed by callous parish overseers of almshouses. Slavery was more protean and pervasive in Britain than many realised. There was no protection for John Hudson and no trade union to regulate his working conditions. One observer in 1784 succinctly captured the national hypocrisy:

> While our pride is flattered by the idea of relieving slaves abroad, we make a set of our fellow-subjects at home infinitely greater slaves, and far more miserable! This is something like the fashionable chimera of universal philanthropy, which pretends to be alive to the sufferings of the distant Hottentots but in reality steels the heart against spectacles of much keener wretchedness in our own streets.[23]

Coincidentally, the very year that Hudson landed in Australia was also that in which the first British legislation designed to alleviate the lot of the chimneysweeps was passed, despite considerable parliamentary opposition. It seems highly likely that this opposition was generated by a fear that it could release many destitute boys onto their parishes for relief. As a result, property was placed ahead of humanity and the actual effect of the act was negligible. What is significant, however, is the evidence that public interest and sentiment were growing. Chimneysweeps were becoming objects of special concern.

This special concern is best known to us today via two of William Blake's most poignant poems. Both are entitled 'The Chimney Sweeper' from the *Songs of Innocence* and *Songs of Experience*, first published together in 1794. Together they provide a moving portrait of the hardship that John Hudson endured:

> When my mother died I was very young,
> And my father sold me while yet my tongue,
> Could scarcely cry weep, weep, weep, weep.
> So your chimneys I sweep & in soot I sleep.[24]

In its companion verse we see the young chimneysweep through Blake's genius as an illustrator. The boy is around John Hudson's own age. Barefoot in the snow with a blackened face, he is carrying a bag of soot and a wire brush. The doors and windows of the houses he passes are all shut. He is an outcast. The bleak situation is also indicative of the chill of parental neglect and the cold heart of society. For Blake, the fate of these young chimneysweeps was to be children without a childhood. It was an occupation which was the very analogy of death itself when chimneys could become 'coffins of black'.

PERCEPTIONS OF CHILDHOOD

TO the poor, childhood was a luxury they could not afford.

Fifty years earlier, in 1729 and across the water in Dublin, the sixty-two-year-old dean of St Patrick's Cathedral sat down to a solitary meal. He felt bereft of friends and far from the intellectual stimuli of London. Although an Irish national hero, Dean Jonathan Swift had no-one to act as hostess of the deanery since his beloved neighbour Stella died the year before. The coffee houses of London where the leading wits and satirists of the day welcomed him as master were far away. He was increasingly subject to deafness, giddiness and overpowering noises in the head: his decay of flesh was matched by a decay of dreams and ambitions.

Outside, on the streets of Dublin, the lower classes seemed bred for upper-class consumers; children were neglected and starved, babies abandoned. And as Dean Swift sat down he ruminated on another means of dealing with the growing numbers of the poor, of 'a young healthy Child...a year old, a most delicious, nourishing, and wholesome Food; whether Stewed, Roasted, or Boiled'.[1] This was not madness. Swift's thoughts on the poor and their children had led to this inescapable satrical 'solution'. In this calm and considered recipe was his modest proposal for the 120,000 children born annually to the Irish poor. Other advantages Swift foresaw and appropriated to his argument were that this would result in an increase in marital affection and motherly love: 'Men would become as fond of their wives, during the Time of their Pregnancy, as...of their Mares in Foal... and it would prevent those voluntary Abortions, and that horrid Practice of Women murdering their Bastard Children.'[2]

This monstrous inversion of values—of children as food, of horses valued over wives and of mothers as murderers—was part of a shocking and sustained squib on eighteenth-century British attitudes and neglect. 'A Modest Proposal' remains unsettling for the rational and convincing power of its argument. And yet, how far removed from reality were Swift's visions of parents selling their children, of wives as chattels and of the lower classes as a consumer product?

Swift's vision of market forces driving society was as relevant fifty years later and for that generation of children who sailed on the First Fleet. In 1779 the most widely read work of the day on the history and condition of women in Britain, William Alexander's *The History of Women*, asserted that the nation still gave more attention to breeding horses and puppies than to children.[3] And in 1785 Jonas Hanway wrote of children being sold for less than the price of a puppy: 'Orphans...or the illegitimate children of the poorest kind of people are said to be sold; that is, their service for seven years is disposed of for twenty or thirty shillings; being a smaller price than the value of a terrier.'[4] Children, and not just poor children, were still regarded as a commodity, as economic objects. Even more fortunate children from the upper classes were 'sold' into advantageous marriages and bought dynastic alliances of wealth, position and power.

What had changed, however, was the anthropological interest in the lives of the impoverished, and a growing concern to document mortality rates and parish expenditures in an effort to underpin proposals for relief and reform. As Britain moved towards 1787, the growth of publications, proposals, addresses, exhortations, remedies and charitable solutions to the problem of the burgeoning poor turned into an avalanche. Some of this was prompted by genuine philanthropic concern; some was more clearly generated by self-preservation, by an upper-class fear of revolution and riot. By the end of the century, voicing opinions about the condition of the poor was as fashionable a conversational gambit as art, music and literature. But on the eve of the departure of the First Fleet what *was* the popular concept of childhood, and what did concepts like family and motherhood mean?

Childhood and parenthood are socially constructed ideas and culture-specific. Late eighteenth-century concepts of childhood and family, and of attitudes to nurturing, were inevitably of their time and different from many of ours today. Most historians accept that during the period of English history from 1660 to 1800 there was a remarkable and positive change in attitudes to children and to family life, at least among the landed and professional classes. At these levels of society the family supposedly became more child-oriented and affectionate, with a recognition of the uniqueness of each child.

Before this period there was little concept of childhood at all. The formality of family relationships meant that parents were distant, unapproachable beings and children were inferior objects owing them diffidence and unquestioning obedience. As the capacity for affection developed, families began to share more pursuits together. According to the modern historian Randolph

Trumbach 'eighteenth-century parents were just discovering child-hood and learning to enjoy its innocence'.[5]

Almost all histories, however, only uncover middle- and upper-class childhoods and, although their range of source materials is extensive, do not necessarily reveal the actual experience of child-hood. Diaries, letters and first-hand accounts by children themselves are rare and when we attempt to uncover the childhood history of the (often) illiterate poor, we find that attitudes replace actuality. And at this level of society the records are almost exclusively derived from superior and philanthropic viewpoints. The poor are rarely witnesses for themselves. In 1788 the Reverend J. Howlett placed these class differences into an ageless context:

> It is remarkable, that as every age deems the present more wicked than the preceding ones; so, on the contrary every rank and order of society seem to look upon their own as the best and most virtuous of all. The higher orders think themselves alone possessed of every excellence, and regard the lower as vile and contemptible, destitute of every principle of honour and honesty, and prone to whatever is base and worthless. The latter, in their turn, are equally conceited, and look upon the former as proud and haughty and insolent, cruel, oppressive and tyranni-cal. The middle classes, mean time, are not a whit behind either; but consider both those above and those beneath them as equally vicious and profligate, and as equally objects of dislike and aversion. Hence it is that the sentiments of all, respecting each other, are commonly false and erroneous.[6]

Most modern historians present the poor as much less subject to an evolution in attitude towards children—they are said to have adhered to patterns of neglect and cruelty towards their offspring long after substantial changes in other classes occurred: 'There are levels of human misery at which the intensity of the struggle to satisfy the basic need for food and shelter leaves little room for humane emotions and affective relationships.'[7]

One of the dangers inherent in viewing history as a constant linear development is that the eighteenth-century poor would be seen as anthropological misfits without fully developed emotions, who only grudgingly evolved into civilised adults: 'Among the mass of the very poor, the available evidence suggests that the common behaviour of many parents towards their children was often indifferent, cruel, erratic and unpredictable,' though this may partly be excused 'because they needed to vent their frustration on somebody.'[8]

These opinions serve to imitate the ideology and sensibility of eighteenth-century upper-class paternalists.[9] Many historians have concentrated on punishment to the exclusion of many other childhood experiences, and by using late-twentieth-century criteria on child care it is often possible to overstate the brutal past. The context of the times must always be at the forefront of thinking when evaluating social behaviour.

Other twentieth-century historians believe that the concept of childhood is not a modern phenomena; that affective family groups have long existed and that a concentration on punishment and discipline has been to the neglect of other childhood experiences. Even so, the opinion that 'the majority of children were not subjected to brutality' still seems questionable.[10]

Perhaps both sides overstate their case, but the majority of the population at this time were living poor or destitute lives. If their children weren't subjected to brutality in the home they most probably were outside it. Employers and masters preyed on children and the brutality of neglect and indifference by their 'betters' made them a race apart.

In the 1970s Lloyd de Mause wrote, 'the further back in history one goes, the lower the level of child care, and the more likely children are to be killed, abandoned, beaten, terrorised, and sexually abused'.[11] The validity of this controversial and ugly vision remains a subject for debate. What cannot be gainsaid, though, is the appalling mortality rate for infants and young children in the eighteenth century. And this scourge spared neither commoner nor aristocrat: of Queen Anne's seventeen pregnancies in sixteen years, ten ended in miscarriage and only one child survived infancy.

Infants and children under five accounted for almost half of all deaths in London in the mid-eighteenth century, and it was not until the 1790s that an excess of births over deaths began to occur regularly. By the end of the century Swift's vision of an inhuman food chain moved into a modern idiom, with the city as a devouring Moloch voraciously consuming infants and young children. Those who had not succumbed to convulsions, tetanus, diarrhoea, gripes, atrophy, infantile scurvy, pneumonia or whooping cough were then exposed to various communicable diseases such as diphtheria, smallpox, scarlet fever, measles, tuberculosis and epidemic meningitis, or to nutritional disorders like rickets. This obstacle course was further compounded by ignorance, neglect, cruelty and abandonment, and with only the most rudimentary paediatric knowledge to counter the suffering. Thus a lack of effective contraception together with contaminated water supplies and a gross disregard for hygiene were combined with an ignorance of childbirth techniques and inadequate antenatal care.

Superstition and folklore still exerted a strong influence on many, and an oral tradition offered both dubious as well as valuable assistance. It was believed, for example, that there was an alarming crossover between the visual world and the developing foetus: if a pregnant woman were to see a snake the baby would have green eyes, or if she saw a hare the baby would have a hare lip. The most extraordinary superstitions connected with the diet of pregnant women and infants remained popular as well. As late as 1784 an English traveller in France was surprised to find that the abundance of strawberries and lobsters in that country's diet did not produce a crop of strawberry marks and deformed claw-like hands among the children of mothers who indulged themselves in such treats while they were pregnant.[12] And earlier in the century the custom of feeding a day-old baby on roast pork 'to cure it of all the Mother's Longings' took a long time to die out.[13]

One famous instance of the contradictions of this time, of society's developments in science and medicine compromised by its reluctance to forgo entrenched superstitious beliefs, is the case of Mary Toft. Early in the 1700s Mary Toft was supposedly sitting in a field, whereupon she was frightened by a rabbit. Soon after, she claimed to have given birth to one of these creatures and went on to become a celebrated public talking point as these 'births' continued. Her claims were much publicised, through the popular press as well as word of mouth. The royal court was interested enough to send a representative who confirmed the births, and Hogarth commemorated the event in an engraving.

Another practice which contributed to the high mortality among infants and young children was the fashion of sending infants away soon after birth to be suckled by surrogate mothers. Nursing and baby care were considered too debilitating and coarse for ladies of fashion and breeding and for these reasons women from the lower classes were used as wet-nurses. By the very end of the century, however, it had become increasingly fashionable for gentlewomen to suckle their own children.

Paediatrics as a specialised field of medicine was a mid-eighteenth-century development. Before this time any medical texts on the subject were written in Latin and were intended for physicians rather than mothers and families. Many were compendiums of long-held beliefs, untested against more modern conditions, that contradicted new discoveries and improved diagnostic skills. The first best-selling manual intended for a wide public circulation was William Buchan's *Domestic Medicine: The Family's Physician* in 1769. Buchan wrote this work based on his experiences as physician at a foundling hospital outside London. Although no mention is made of specific medical texts in the journals and writings of First Fleet surgeons, this is one work likely to have made the journey. It was an immediate success on first publication, and was reprinted into the next century and issued in America as well as in translation all over Europe. By the time it reached its ninth edition in 1784 the work was celebrated enough to include a dedication to Sir Joseph Banks and later earned its author a resting place in Westminster Abbey.

Before 1750 the care of infants had been left to old women, nurses and midwives. Even after male physicians began to annex this new medical territory it was reported that many were clearly 'not fond of practising among infants...[and] make no scruple to assert that there is nothing to be done for children when they are ill'.[14] It might seem that an extreme infant mortality rate made physicians rather less than caring. Certainly there has been a twentieth-century inference that parents in the past limited their emotional investment in children whose life expectations were low. Such an example is found in Dr Johnson's cold comfort to his friend James Boswell, on the death of Boswell's young son: 'You must remember that to keep three out of four is more than your share.' George Armstrong, an early children's specialist in London, who had written a popular paediatric textbook declared: 'Children while in their infancy, especially if the young family is numerous, and the parents in straitened circumstances, are not thought of sufficient consequence to be much attended to, unless some sudden or violent illness happens to give an alarm.'[15]

The mortality rate, and the philanthropic and medical attention it received as the century progressed, is central to any discussion of child care, the quality of childhood and of the emotional life of families at this time. All this should be seen in an eighteenth-century context with its emphasis on parental respect, on deference and obligation. Affection and sentimental attachments were mostly treated with suspicion and thought to lead to disorder and instability.

In the world of the poor and the destitute, unwanted children were abandoned in the street or left in secluded spots where they would die of exposure. Some were dumped on the doorsteps of wealthy families in the hope that they would offer charity to the foundling. The workhouse was another possibility, although leaving infants to its care was usually tantamount to murder by neglect. In a well-known work of the time, 'The State of the Poor, or an History of the Labouring Classes in England', Frederick Morton Eden wrote:

> It is, perhaps, not an unnatural course for a mother to abandon her child to the parish-officers, who, she is assured, will provide for it, (for some years at least,) better than she possibly could; more particularly, when that child is the fruit of an illicit connexion, and when, by leaving it at the work-house, she can often screen her character from detection.[16]

Foundling hospitals were the first large-scale practical attempt to counter this infant mortality rate, with the first opening in London in 1741. Before this the public was more concerned with punishing the guilty mother than with helping her innocent offspring, and crowds would flock to see convicted whores stripped to the waist and whipped. There was also opposition to these hospitals from people who thought that the existence of such charities would serve to encourage sexual irresponsibility and increase the problem of unwanted births. Dorothy George writes:

> No expedient has yet been found out for preventing the murder of poor miserable infants at their birth, or suppressing the inhuman custom of exposing newly born infants to perish in the streets; or the putting of such unhappy foundlings to wicked and barbarous nurses, who undertake to bring them up for a small and trifling sum of money, do often suffer them to starve for want of due sustenance or care, or if permitted to live either turn them into the streets to beg or steal, or hire them out to loose persons by whom they are trained up in that infamous way of living and sometimes are blinded or maimed and distorted in their limbs in order to move pity or compassion, and thereby become fitter instruments of gain to those vile and merciless wretches.[17]

By 1753 over a hundred infants a day were being offered to the London Foundling Hospital. As a result of this, the hospital's physician William Cadogan found it necessary to write a directive for his nursing staff in 1748 titled 'Essay upon Nursing, and the Management of Children'. With such initiatives the death rate dropped almost 50 per cent only to rise alarmingly when parliament offered to support the cost of wholesale admissions. Some two-thirds of the 15,000 babies brought to the hospital between 1756 and 1761 died.

Changing accepted attitudes to the God-given status and role of the poor in society was fundamental if they were to enjoy any improvements in their lives. Through the founding of this hospital and in the efforts of figures like philanthropist Jonas Hanway, we can see that a new attitude of the poor was emerging—that their condition was a result of unjust laws, appalling environments and lack of general education rather than original sin or an inscrutable Providence.

The charities of London underwent a remarkable transformation between the beginning of the Seven Years War in 1756, and the end of the American Revolution in 1783, and the shift in humanitarian concern was related to these events. The first war provoked apprehension that the British population was inadequate to meet European conflict and competition, while the second deprived Britain of a great potential reservoir of seamen, soldiers and manpower. A new attitude that considered the British poor and their children as a national resource was being voiced—an attitude best exemplified in Hanway's writings.

Hanway was 'the most versatile and effective philanthropist of his time' who attacked checks on population from whatever quarter they came: dangers of using wet nurses, the hazards of swaddling infants, the housing of children with dissolute parents, infant mortality.[18] He also had more eccentric claims to fame. Despite public derision, he carried an umbrella through the streets of London for thirty years until he made the usage popular. Later still, he incurred Dr Johnson's wrath by estimating that the poor spent too much money on drinking tea. Apart from these endearing foibles, Hanway promoted numerous philanthropic schemes and became the champion of the chimneysweeps.

Hanway's investigations into the infant mortality rate revealed a large number of foundlings, most of whom were illegitimate. Radical demographic changes at the time account for this sudden increase. Before mid-century, England was a patchwork of distinct and separate local communities, within which the great majority lived and died close to the places where they had been born, knowing very little of other communities. After the 1750s, however, thousands of labourers moved across the country, attracted to London and to the new industrial centres in particular. By the end of the century Frederick Eden commented that 'if a husband-labourer has four or five children, it rarely happens that above three of them settle where they were born'.[19] The result was that 'in London at least three-quarters of the inhabitants are strangers'.[20]

One of the most familiar archetypes of the time was the figure of the wholesome and innocent country girl who came to London looking for honest work and finished up as a whore. A 1787 manual of morals and training contained the dire warning: 'You had better turn your daughter into the street, at once, than place her out to service. For ten to one her master shall seduce her, or she shall be made the "confidante" of her mistress's intrigues.'[21]

This wholesale migration contributed to the increase in illegitimacy which began in the early 1700s and rose sharply after 1750 in every city on the continent as well as in Britain.[22] The external controls over courtship and marriage, which for many couples involved some element of premarital cohabitation, could hardly be part of transient urban situations. Traditional controls from families, local communities and the church which had ensured that marriages occurred were being broken.[23]

London, of course, attracted more than the itinerant labourer, the naive country girl and the adventurer. Aristocratic preferment could only be obtained by regular attendance at Court and the pleasures of the metropolis exerted a strong attraction on the gentry. Commentators in the 1780s deplored the breakdown of village life and its benign paternalism:

> Persons of fortune so generally flock to great towns to spend their money and their time, wantoning in city pleasures [and thereby] abandon the humble villager.
>
> There are many gentlemen of landed estates, who,

it is well known, hardly ever visit their village, though they might live like little sovereigns on their own domain, blessed, and blessing all their dependents round them...If city pleasures absorb the thoughts of so many, and direct them from rustic duties and village benevolence, we may deplore the evil we cannot cure.[24]

Rapid social change was occurring and left in its path a nostalgia for the supposed simplicity and virtues of village life. In 1770 Oliver Goldsmith published his poem 'The Deserted Village', in which he lamented the passing of the old pattern of agrarian life. He suggested that in times gone by the peasantry and yeomanry of old England had been the country's pride: each man had his plot of land and each lord his sense of responsibility, always ready both to punish and to protect those who were dependent upon him. This rural paradise was now being eroded by the capitalistic greed of the new landowners, who were breaking up the old village lands in order to establish for themselves great enclosed estates. The result was that England was becoming a country of landless labourers, many of them dependent on daily wages to keep them and their families out of the workhouse.[25] The popular attitude to this change was that peasantry of the old sort had been a guarantee of stability, whereas an independent body of landless labourers seemed to menace the prosperity as well as the security of the realm.

By the end of the eighteenth century, by John Hudson's time in fact, this national security seemed to be at breaking point. English gaols were perilously overcrowded. In 1784, the year after John Hudson was sentenced, the number of trials at the Old Bailey reached its peak and in 1785 capital convictions reached the highest point in the decade. Crime was rampant. New places of criminal exile were necessarily and anxiously assessed. In

August 1786 Botany Bay was settled upon as a new venue for convict exile. This was to be John Hudson's destination.

Convict transportation. Exile from home. Banishment overseas. Seventeen eighty-eight was but one landmark year in this centuries-old process. While different times may have favoured one term over another the truth is that the British parliament had empowered magistrates to exile malefactors 'beyond the seas' as early as 1597. By 1615 King James I was authorising pardons for condemned felons on condition of banishment to the new American colonies. The Virginia Company, which had suggested to the burghers of the City of London that unwanted children would be welcome in the American colonies, received 100 such child migrants in 1620. This was not an entirely philanthropic gesture but a way for eager parishes to off-load pauper children from their ratepayers' charity lists and for the colonies to acquire a new work force which also swelled the numbers of their British population. Twenty years later, in 1640, a London alderman left a bequest of money to be used expressly for 'poore Boyes and Girles to be taken up out of the streets of London as Vagrants for the Cloathing and transporting of them to Virginia, New England or any other of the Western Plantations'.[26] Eighty years later, in 1718, the Transportation Act formalised the punishment in its evolution from a sporadic and haphazard practice to a highly complex and institutionalised procedure. Thereafter, perhaps as many as 50,000 British subjects were transported to America and the West Indies until the War of American Independence brought an abrupt halt to such traffic in 1775.

By the time peace was restored a decade later British gaols were so overcrowded that they were a threat to national security as well as public health. According to one estimate the prison population

had swollen by an alarming 73 per cent. When convict transportation to Australia became a viable alternative it was
continuing a tradition of 250 years.

What was John Hudson's reaction to a sentence of transportation
rather than the death penalty? Did he appreciate the 'leniency' of
his sentence? Like most Londoners, Hudson had presumably
witnessed public executions: they were the most popular mass
spectacle of the day and attracted up to 80,000 spectators at a
time. The lawmakers and propertied elite believed that such
spectacles had a sobering effect upon the criminal class. Yet the
truth is that all too often these public executions became a means
whereby the mob defied authority and turned the guilty into
momentary folk heroes. In 1772, one observer described the effect
of these executions upon an audience which saw death as 'nothing
more than a wry face and a watered patch of breeches'.[27] In the
same year it was observed that parents took their children to a
hanging and then flogged them afterwards 'that they might
remember the example they had seen'.[28]

Before we continue to trace our chimneysweep's circuitous path
to the Australian colony in 1788, we can find further insights into
the world of the abandoned children and the criminal poor in
John Hudson's court record. Consider the evidence of the pawnbroker in Hudson's case and the role of the pawnshop in the world
of the destitute and the desperate: 'I am a pawnbroker, on the
17th of October, the boy at the bar brought this shirt to pledge
about seven in the morning; he said it belonged to his father, I
asked him who sent him with it, he said, his mother.'[29]

Almost anything could be turned to account at the pawnbrokers. Like John Hudson, a significant number of those who
were to become First Fleeters attempted to pawn stolen goods. It

was not necessary to have arcane contacts: pawnshops were everywhere and in many cases the pawnbroker should have been called a receiver. And if, instead of 1783, the year had been 1838, then John Hudson could easily have been one of the young thieves in *Oliver Twist* whose precarious existence depended upon the services of such receivers.

The ubiquitous presence of pawnbrokers is an interesting contrast to the absence of an effective police force at the time. When John Hudson was apprehended, the population of London was nearing one million and yet it had no centralised police force to oversee this vast domain. Each parish maintained officers who were responsible to local magistrates. The most significant development had been the establishment of the Bow Street Runners in 1749. But parliamentary funding and support for such innovations were intermittent and eighteenth-century citizens were forced to form vigilante groups for the protection of life and property. In 1785 a bill before parliament sought to establish a united and national police force similar to that in France, yet the bill foundered—partly on the belief that such a system was too foreign for England. Another fifty years were to pass before London had an effective, centralised police force which would create official crime records and make the gathering of evidence a professional rather than a public activity.[30]

In John Hudson's case this gathering of evidence was solely the work of the householder himself. Witness his testimony:

> I found upon the window shutter the marks...as if somebody had slided down the window...I observed a table that stood very near the window, there I found the mark of sooty feet...I took the impressions...upon a piece of paper as minutely as I could...the boy denied the robbery till the time that he was examined by this piece of paper, and then he acknowledged it.[31]

It is extraordinary to imagine that if John Hudson had washed before the robbery there would have been no telltale prints and no householder's evidence that linked him to the crime. His fate was decided by something so easily overlooked, yet something so damning, and it was this oversight that led him to the horrors of Newgate.

NEWGATE PRISON—AN
ENTRANCE TO HELL

WHEN philanthropists and early prison reformers described English gaols as 'nurseries of crime' they were assessing the unhealthy environment which indiscriminately housed hardened criminals with young offenders.[1] The result was a prison society which tutored these young inmates into a fully fledged criminal future. John Howard, the famous advocate of social reform, wrote: 'In some Gaols you see...boys...eagerly listening to the stories told by practised and experienced criminals, of their adventures, successes, stratagems, and escapes.'[2]

The term 'nurseries' was particularly apt at yet another level of interpretation: free children with their convicted parent or parents were a common and accepted part of the daily life of many eighteenth-century prisons. Some of these children accompanied a parent (usually the mother) to gaol, some were born in the gaol, and others were conceived within the prison walls. To all such children prison was indeed a nursery, although it hardly conformed to expectations as a suitable place in which to raise the young.

The unrestricted intermingling of the sexes within the confines of prisons meant that about half of the convicts' children who embarked on the First Fleet had been conceived and born behind bars. At least a dozen children of convict mothers who were to sail on the First Fleet arrived at or were born in a prison—Gloucester, Lincoln, Manchester, Norwich, Winchester and, for the majority, Newgate Prison. And those children who accompanied their convict mothers to gaol were sometimes incarcerated for up to two years before delivery onto the First Fleet—such was the case with Mary Fowles. Hannah Mullens was one mother under sentence of death who waited over eight months before her sentence was changed to transportation. During these months Mullens was presumably held in a cell for condemned prisoners together with a child, who shared the hideous uncertainty of her mother's life.

Furthermore, a number of the women convicts were pregnant at the time of embarkation on 13 May 1787 and were to give birth on the way to Botany Bay. Some had conceived in prison; other pregnancies were the result of liaisons with sailors of the Fleet in the months following the women's transfer from prisons to the ships. These facts, to some, confirmed the belief that the women convicts were abandoned and immoral characters. A more considered interpretation would be that these desperate and frightened women formed liaisons in a search for affection, for protection, for a future and a role beyond that of mere convict.

Eighteenth-century prisons were run on a private-enterprise basis where the governor, turnkeys and staff profited from renting out superior accommodation, selling liquor, procuring sexual favours, charging admission fees to a curious public, accepting bribes and compiling pamphlets for sale on the most notorious prisoners and their public executions. When Richard Akerman died in 1792 he had held office as the keeper of Newgate for thirty-eight years, and the £20,000 fortune that he left illustrates the lucrative nature of his position. Women prisoners were more likely to be impoverished than their male counterparts and less able to afford anything extra to alleviate their situation. The major difference between the sexes in the gaols was that women had a better chance of receiving last-minute pardons, and if this failed there was always the short-term reprieve from 'pleading their belly'.

The most astounding thing about prison life at the time was its domesticity. The wives and even the children of prisoners sometimes managed to stay overnight and affluent prisoners could pay a fee to have their families reside in Newgate. The social life of the prison was further enhanced by frequent visitors, and even sight-seers were permitted to come and go at will: 'visitors thronged into the gaol to comfort the prisoners and supply them with food, money, drink and other necessities'.[3]

The British prison system, particularly in London, began to show acute strain during the mid-eighteenth-century crime wave that followed demobilisation after the War of the Austrian Succession. With prisons overwhelmed by the crush of poor awaiting trial for petty property crime it was no wonder that typhus (gaol fever) became a terrible risk. In April 1750, two diseased prisoners from Newgate Prison facing trial in the Old Bailey managed to infect the entire courtroom. Sixty people died from gaol fever in a single session—and these were not other prisoners. With frightening speed the judge, jury, lawyers and many spectators were struck down. This disaster convinced the Corporation of London that building and sanitary reforms were long overdue. Even so, the new Newgate was not opened until twenty years later in 1770—just in time to cater to the crime wave that followed another demobilisation after the Seven Years War.

Newgate was divided into two halves with affluent prisoners who could pay extortionate prices for better lodging and services on the Master's Side. Typical offences for those imprisoned here were the 'respectable' crimes of libel, sedition or embezzlement. The more impoverished prisoners were held in the charity wards on the Common Side and endured miserable conditions and ill-treatment. Many on this side had to depend on money and food brought in by family and friends. Just how was someone like John Hudson expected to survive?

Prisoners also had access to a taphouse where they could purchase liquor, several community rooms, a chapel, a separate infirmary for men and women and exercise yards. The gaol was chronically overcrowded throughout the century and by the 1780s the number of women prisoners was increasing. These women were vividly described as being 'of the very lowest and most wretched class of human beings, almost naked, with only a few filthy rags almost alive and in motion with vermin, their bodies rotting with the bad distemper, and covered with itch, scorbutic and venereal ulcers'.[4]

So far as the poor and the destitute were concerned, there seemed little to distinguish conditions inside the charity wards of Newgate from those outside. Indeed, any significant difference which improved the prison might have been seen as a positive encouragement to commit crime! The overcrowded tenement slums were huddled side by side with gin-shops and brothels and provided the meanest possible accommodation. Rooms were bare boards, without furniture and beds. In the absence of a sanitary system the poor made a public convenience of any nook or cranny and disease and sickness were rampant. How did this differ from life within Newgate?

The prison was, in fact, a carceral city in its own right, even more crowded in the day when visitors, tradesmen, accomplices

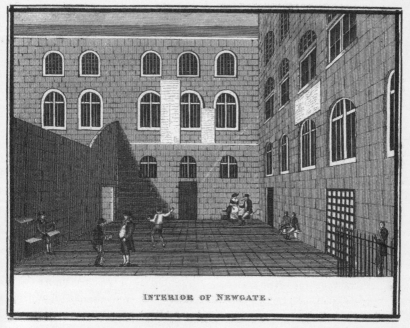

INTERIOR OF NEWGATE.

A late eighteenth-century engraving of the partially rebuilt Newgate Prison in 1783–84. John Hudson was there at this time. Although Hudson was still a child, there was no segregation of the prisoners according to age or offence.

and sightseers had unrestricted access.[5] By law, the gaoler had to provide debtors and criminals with separate sleeping quarters, although everyone still managed to mix by day. The sexes were intermingled, the young with the old, the insane with the weak-minded. Wives managed to hide and stay overnight with their imprisoned husbands, pets were kept, and the taphouse, which eventually became more of a general store where beer and spirits were freely available, was as popular with visitors as it was with the prisoners. Among the daily sightseers who thronged into Newgate were hordes of prostitutes, who plied their trade as freely within Newgate as without—the turnkeys could easily be bribed to turn a blind eye to such excesses. Within this grim carnival the most popular occasions, and the most profitable for the turnkeys, were those days in which the condemned prisoners could be visited.

In the absence of any formal structure for prison services the prisoners had to establish a community life themselves and be self-reliant for cooking, cleaning and caring for the needy. This self-reliance extended to providing entertainment, emotional support, scribes, advisers and midwives. It was an anarchic self-governing gaol with its own robust subculture where drinking, gambling and sex were the only relief to prisoners who had no organised prison labour to occupy their time.

'Indulgences' sold on the Master's Side were the sole source of income for the keepers. But while this made them financially independent of the state, it effectively emancipated them from legal restraint as well. Prison keepers were not the only occupation to operate on such lines: nurses, justices' clerks and constables all existed on fees they could garner for their services. However, no eighteenth-century institution was as chronically under-financed or as subject to abuse as the prison. It consisted of entrenched inmate subcultures, which ensured that abuses occurred, and the very epitome of abuse was present in Newgate. Authority was capricious, arbitrary and unchecked by the outside world. Neither the keeper's authority nor the type of discipline to be enforced was laid down. Both leniency and cruelty could be attributed to the absence of strict and accountable supervision.

Within this community there were at least three groups that required care and attention: the insane, the sick and children. Little was done for all three. The insane were the most dramatic threat to the peace and safety of the prison; they circulated freely and were neglected objects of scorn that were an essential part of the circus for sightseers.

The sick were given only the most rudimentary attention despite the establishment of two infirmaries—for men and women—that were little more than segregated kennels and were unlikely to relieve or comfort the prisoners. There does not seem to have been any medical attention provided for those without family or friends to pay for a visiting physician—and physicians would often refuse to enter the prison for fear their own health would suffer. The only time the keeper was informed of a prisoner's condition was when he received notice to conduct a funeral. The keeper's fundamental duty was to keep his prisoners confined, and his highest aspiration was to wheedle fees out of them or their visitors.

Children were the most likely group to be cared for, although at a very early age it would have been necessary for them to develop habits of self-preservation and self-reliance. The hardships John Hudson experienced outside Newgate, as an orphan chimney-sweep, would have provided him with essential lessons that helped him survive his incarceration.

Feuding, bitterness and intimidation energised many of the inmates who either had a death sentence hanging over them or were already marked for transportation. Quarrels over food, bedding, clothes, barters and loans frequently disrupted daily life and anyone who was not accepted into the prisoners' hierarchy suffered accordingly—the insane, the deformed, the religious, the country inmate whose regional accent marked him as an outsider.

The women had no uniforms to wear, no matron to oversee their needs. There was no allowance for bedding or straw and they slept tightly packed into rows in the women's wards. Until tamed by Elizabeth Fry and her Association for the Improvement of the Female Prisoners in Newgate, founded in 1817, the women's side was much as it had been described in *Moll Flanders* a century earlier. Many of Moll's exploits and the conditions she encountered were based on Defoe's own experiences as a prisoner of

Newgate, and Moll's description of the women's wards seems timeless in its horror:

> tis impossible to describe the terror of my mind, when I was first brought in, and when I looked round upon all the horrors of that dismal place…the hellish noise, the roaring, swearing, and clamour, the stench and nastiness, and all the dreadful crowd of afflicting things that I saw there, joined together to make the place seem an emblem of hell itself, and a kind of an entrance into it.[6]

The first in Moll's list of horrors is the noise of Newgate, which claims her attention even before the prison's stench. Much of this noise came from women who ran towards visitors like hounds in a kennel importuning them for money, for drink, for indulgences and assistance and offering sexual favours in return. The competition to be heard must have been ferocious. This noise was the only way the women could assert themselves—reticence and decorum were not life skills in this place. And, of course, a begging mother holding an infant to her breast was all the more likely to attract compassion and charity in the competing din.

By the middle of the eighteenth century some attempt was made to regulate children accompanying criminal parents into Newgate. Only nursing children were supposed to accompany parents, although there were no nursery facilities available, nor was there any provision for schooling. The frequent alternative to keep children occupied and out of the way was to send them to the workhouse—a highly questionable choice given that in some workhouses the infant mortality rate amounted to a veritable slaughter of the innocents.

Children remained an ignored and undifferentiated part of the prison population until the early nineteenth century when

Elizabeth Fry became the first penal reformer to devote her attention to the plight of imprisoned women and their children. It is significant that her first efforts centred on providing clothing and schooling for these children, and in the 1850s the first purpose-built prison for women was opened in Brixton, London, which included a convict nursery. For any late eighteenth-century mother imprisoned in Newgate with a child the burden was the same within as without the walls: to find clothing, food and warmth for themselves and their offspring.

In 1777, two years after the outbreak of the war between Britain and America, the first exhaustive survey of conditions in English prisons, John Howard's *The State of the Prisons* was published. This comparative survey of English and continental prisons and of the gross deficiencies and abuses on the English side not only encouraged reform and the building of new 'model' prisons but also led to a major change in government attitude. Authorities began to consider solitary confinement and hard labour as an alternative to transportation. While transportation and hanging were to remain major punishments for serious crimes of violence against people and property, prison sentences for minor property crimes were to become a real alternative. Even the Committee of 1785 which argued for the resumption of transportation did so with many misgivings:

> Transportation answers very imperfectly the purpose
> of Example That tho' a transported Convict may
> suffer under his Sentence his sufferings are
> unseen…[and] strike no terror into the minds of those
> for whose correction it was introduced to operate.[7]

The selfless dedication with which John Howard pursued prison reform captured both the public imagination and the ear of authority. His passionate commitment led him to undertake no less than four extensive tours of prisons and bridewells—in Europe one of the few prisons to refuse him admission was the Bastille. So great was the recognised authority of his findings that three editions of his massive survey were published in his own lifetime, with a further issued posthumously.

The scandalous abuses in prison conditions to which Howard was exposed, however, were observed at the cost of much of his own fortune and ultimately of his life: on one of his European surveys he contracted a prison fever and died in southern Russia in 1790 at sixty-four.

Did any of these changes influence the fate or improve the conditions of John Hudson's incarceration? His sentencing occurred at the turning point of new legislation, philanthropic endeavour and public awareness, but the ponderous pace of major change to centuries of tradition and authority would have been far too slow for him to benefit. Hudson exchanged Newgate for a floating prison on the First Fleet. He was then exiled to a strange land on the other side of the world.

A NURSERY OF CRIME

He enters the prison…a boy in years, and a boy
in vice; he departs with a knowledge of the ways
of wickedness.

The Philanthropic Society, 1818

AFTER John Hudson's sentence he was regarded as a convict
rather than a child, and the solicitude that the Old Bailey judge
showed him was the last recorded kindness that we know he
received. At this time government authorities were increasingly
concerned to find a destination for all those sentenced to transportation. Hudson soon fell into the rhythms of prison life while
his companions there plotted rebellion and escape.

When Hudson entered Newgate it had only just been rebuilt
after burning down in 1780. Work was sufficiently advanced for
prisoners to be admitted by 1782 and when he entered the gaol
for his four-month stay it was as overcrowded as ever. It may have
been the new Newgate but it was still synonymous with suffering,
despair, viciousness and death.

Behind its forbidding and solemn facade there were still
wretched kennels of cells. Its massive granite walls, strong enough

to resist artillery, frowned down upon the public from the narrow slits of its windows. But if it was alarming to someone on the outside it had an even more pernicious effect on those incarcerated within. The London Grand Jury's verdict of 1820 stated that 'in their opinion, the alarming increase of Crime in the Metropolis, especially among the Juvenile Offenders, is to be chiefly attributed to the very inadequate state of Newgate prison…where boys and girls…are found to associate with the basest and most hardened felons'.[1]

The great prison reformer John Howard revisited the new gaol in 1783 and incorporated his findings into the third edition of his classic work. This was contemporaneous with Hudson's stay in Newgate and there was little that Howard found favourable. He was particularly concerned 'that without more than ordinary care, the prisoners…will be in great danger of the gaol-fever'.[2] Unlike many other gaols, Newgate at least had an infirmary. Even so, it was 'a wretched place' where the dying were 'without hardly any human comfort'.[3]

The experiences of a young offender like John Hudson have been graphically described in reports from a philanthropic group concerned with the reformation of juvenile offenders. These reports provide the most likely indication of Hudson's fate before separate accommodation and consideration were given to criminal children:

> He enters the prison, young in vice, alarmed at the gloom of the cells, terrified with the clank of the irons…There is no classification according to the nature of offences and the degree of guilt. He is immediately thrown amongst the veterans in crime; his fears are derided, his rising repentance subdued, his vicious propensities cherished and inflamed. Here he finds able and willing tutors in all the varieties of

crime, and the very foundations of virtue are utterly sapped and destroyed…His errors may have arisen from the want of instruction; and his great defect may have been that he was ignorant. So he must remain— of virtues at least—for the prison furnishes no means of education, no knowledge but of vice. Idleness may have been the cause of his deserting the paths of virtue; the remedy of a London gaol is the impossibility of obtaining any employment, save what a pack of cards, or a game of chance, may haply afford him…Prisons become the nurseries of crime.[4]

So our young prisoner was confined in what was possibly the only 'nursery' he ever knew—the very antithesis of what a nursery should be. John Hudson was kept with the poor prisoners lodged in the charity wards on the Common Side of Newgate. Here he was expected to exist on the prison issue of a three-half-penny loaf supplemented by charitable donations and the sheriff's weekly meat supply.[5] Without anything to barter, with nothing that could be extorted or stolen from him, with no-one to see after his well-being, Hudson was of no interest to the turnkeys of Newgate. He faced severe malnourishment, brutality, depravity and lack of medical care. Furthermore, his prison term spanned an English winter—a guarantee of intensified sufferings. One horrified visitor to Newgate in 1786 observed: 'I saw many poor miserable objects almost naked, without shoes or stockings. I fear this winter, if not relieved, the toes of many of them will rot off.'[6]

The threat of disease and suffering that John Hudson faced would have been matched by an equally dangerous moral contagion. John was undoubtedly part of the subculture in Newgate Prison: one of depravity, profanity, wretchedness and degradation. In spite of the intermingling of the sexes and opportunities for heterosexual liaisons, there were also opportunities (threats or forcible demands) for an alternative sexual orientation. Some embraced it from previous inclination, some as a temporary expedient. Others, perhaps John, were forced to submit. In 1846 Earl Grey wrote that 'the tendency to unnatural crime, fostered as it must be when numbers of one sex are congregated together, though checked by material obstacles, will in all probability break out when the convict is released from controul and seeks its indulgence'.[7]

All in all Hudson's living conditions and experiences in Newgate were much the same as if he were still at large. And perhaps that was why he survived.

Even before the First Fleet left England, Captain Phillip displayed an awareness of the sexual danger in confining so many men together and issued his strongest warning—a threat that was as frightening as it was savage. He viewed sodomy as a crime that warranted death and proposed to deliver any culprit to the natives of New Zealand 'and let them eat him'.[8] Although there is no proof that John was a victim of homosexual rape, his later confinement on Norfolk Island certainly exposed him to this threat.

At 7 a.m. on 30 March 1784, John was expelled from the prison. He was one of about ninety convicts sent to the transport ship the *Mercury* which was moored in the Thames. In the company of another young convict (James Grace, who may have been as young as eleven) and upwards of twenty women and girls, Hudson entered the next stage of his sentence.

The chance to walk, or at least to shuffle, in the open air and down to the river on this early spring morning was surely a welcome diversion—a blessed release from the fetid atmosphere of Newgate Prison. This excursion cannot have been much different from that depicted in an illustration hidden in the set of published criminal records known as the *Newgate Calendar*. On the

The CONVICTS taking Water near Black-Friars Bridge,
in order for their being conveyed to WOOLWICH.

In the early morning of 30 March 1784 John Hudson, chained and in the company of about ninety other convicts, was sent from Newgate to the transport ship the *Mercury*, which was moored in the Thames—a very similar occurrence to that depicted in this engraving by William Jackson, published in the mid-1790s.

right-hand side of the illustration the elegant arches of Blackfriar's Bridge recede with symmetrical exactitude into the middle-distance. This part of London had been much improved since John Hudson was born. The streets were 'much better paved and lighted than they were formerly...spacious, regular, and airy...The bridge at Blackfriars is a noble monument of taste and public spirit.'[9]

Yet notwithstanding these improvements, the capital was still seen as 'an overgrown monster'.[10] In the illustration of Blackfriars Bridge, and with no pretence to elegance or symmetry, a motley procession of convicts enters chained in a line from neck to neck. The line of adult convicts, is broken by the presence of two small figures yoked together instead of being joined to the rest of the prisoners. One of the boys looks back over his shoulder with a direct stare which has the power to engage the viewer even today. This could almost be John Hudson and James Grace en route to the *Mercury* and transportation to the former American colonies in 1784.

After the War of American Independence erupted in 1775, the British imagined that the conflict would be settled in their favour within two years, and gave little thought to their swelling prison population. As the war dragged on, however, various local remedies were suggested: a plan to build a whole series of new prisons was broached but never eventuated. Africa was then considered as a possible destination and in 1781 the British government provided the African Company with convicts to help garrison its forts on the equatorial west coast—only 15 per cent were still alive one year later. In 1782 another contingent arrived there and it too was decimated by disease.

Then, in August 1783, and with astounding British effrontery, a convict ship was sent to America before a peace treaty had been signed. The convicts wrested control of the *Swift* from the crew even before it had left the English Channel. Some escaped into the English countryside while the remainder continued their voyage and landed in America.

John Hudson travelled on the *Mercury*, the second and last of these attempts to send ships to America without permission the following year. Again it was so ill-conceived and inept that it encouraged another convict overthrow of the vessel. And once again a desperate and determined band of convicts was able to break out of their chains and take over the ship before leaving the Channel. These two mutinies were a great shock to the country and helped undermine any sense of national security. Jonas Hanway described it as 'so shocking to common sense, that if the event were not notorious, beyond concealment, it would be an indecency to mention it'.[11]

For the 179 convicts on board the *Mercury* one wonders if their fear of a savage landfall was as much a goad to mutiny as the successful precedent the previous year.[12] Another inspiring example must have been that offered by the rebellious American colonists themselves. John Hudson, of course, played no central role in these events yet was caught up in the unfolding drama. Although we may never know just how involved he was in the mutiny and escape, he did not remain on the *Mercury* but fled with those who had become, for better or worse, his companions, even his new family.

The *Mercury* left the Thames for Georgia on 2 April 1784. On the morning of 8 April, after a fierce fight with the captain and crew, the convicts seized the ship. They threw their fetters overboard and, after breaking into the wine supplies, vandalised the vessel in a drunken rampage. At one stage it was proposed to cut off the captain's ears—scissors were put to his head before decency prevailed. For six days the desperate band wondered what to do with their new-found freedom.

At first they steered for Ireland and then changed course for Spain, but for all their enterprise and bravado they were unable to make the most of their new command. Finally, they had to release some of the crew to man the distressed ship as drunkenness and nautical ignorance thwarted their escape. On 13 April they entered Torbay Harbour in Devon and that night about forty convicts (men and women) went ashore. Early the next morning two small boats left the *Mercury* with a further sixty-six convicts. Included in this desperate and hopeless flight were nine-year-old John Hudson and eleven-year-old James Grace.

Once again the convicts failed to make the most of their opportunity and the unforeseen presence of one of His Majesty's sloops swiftly brought their escape attempt to an end: a few shots fired by the HMS *Helena* and the mutiny was over. Hudson and his companions were captured and held overnight, moored under the *Helena*'s stern and well guarded. All were sent to Exeter gaol on 15 April. The fact that they were captured before they reached land meant that by a legal technicality they could not be tried for return from transportation—'they were taken on the water, and therefore could not be said to be at large in the kingdom'.[13] On 24 May, a special commission remanded the convicts to their former orders without trial. Those who had reached land were recaptured over the ensuing weeks with at least five found as far away as London. This group *was* guilty of 'return from transportation' and were duly tried and sentenced to the mandatory death penalty, which was then commuted to transportation for life.

A final footnote to the whole sorry episode concerns the fate of the convicts who remained on board during the mutiny. Remarkably, the ship continued on its voyage but, unlike its predecessor the *Swift*, was refused landing in America. The convicts' worst fears were realised when they were literally dumped by the private contractors in Honduras and on the Mosquito Coast!

Hudson had escaped a dreadful fate. Together with most of the other *Mercury* escapees he spent five weeks in Exeter High Gaol, until the prisoners' situation was revealed. Lord Sydney, in a letter to the admiralty, wrote:

> The Gaol at Exeter being so extremely crowded from the number of convicts confined in it, that, exclusive of the danger of their Escape from thence, there is the greatest reason to apprehend that infectious Distempers will break out among them unless they are immediately removed.[14]

The prisoners were presumably packed into Exeter's 'night-dungeons' which were about 20 feet x $12^1/_2$ feet (6 x 3.8 metres). Their subterranean position rendered them a health hazard, although the desire to remove unwelcome guests who were an expense to the county was also part of the concern. Within a month the prisoners were transferred to the *Dunkirk*, moored off Plymouth. They were first 'examined by an experienced Surgeon or Apothecary' and, being 'free from any putrid or infectious Distemper', were considered fit to be transferred.[15] They travelled overnight, chained and in three wagons, and with their reputation for mutiny there was some real apprehension lest they 'alarm the county'.[16] A guard of soldiers accompanied the group, but despite their presence two convicts escaped in the night.

On his arrival at the *Dunkirk* on 29 June 1784, John Hudson's age was recorded as ten. The authorities were understandably uneasy about this confirmed band of convict troublemakers and keen to see them securely confined. Once they were lodged aboard the ship this nervous haste showed itself in the organisational over-sights and inadequacies borne by the 212 convicts.

The treatment of the women convicts was particularly brutal and must have contributed to the cruel hardening of their sensibility which was such a shock to some First Fleet officers almost

View of the JUSTITIA HULK, with the Convicts at Work, near Woolwich.

A William Jackson engraving of the *Justitia* prison hulk. Its counterpart was the *Dunkirk*, where John Hudson was kept for over two and a half years before his transfer to the First Fleet.

three years later. As soon as the overseer William Cowdry left the *Dunkirk* it was reported that 'the officer, serjeant & the whole Guard has recourse to the women'.[17] Cowdry received only minimal support from the authorities in the establishment and management of the ship. Furthermore, this was the first time women had been incarcerated on a hulk. Such a situation was quite contrary to law, although presumably the government justified it as an emergency measure. The under secretary to the admiralty, Evan Nepean, wrote:

> The Act of Parliament does not justify the Removal
> of Women to the temporary Places of Confinement,
> nor is there any vessel appointed for the reception,
> could it be legally done.[18]

The revolt of the American colonies in 1775 led directly to the massive overcrowding of gaols, by those awaiting transportation. As a result, the Hulks Act was passed in May 1776 and for the first time prisoners were put to hard labour dredging the Thames. This novelty soon became a popular public spectacle and although the hulks were meant to be a temporary expedient, they lasted until the mid-nineteenth century.

The *Dunkirk* was an emergency prison ship and not formally incorporated into the prison hulk system until March 1786. Among the many anomalies under which it existed for the two-year interim, none was as remarkable as the presence of women prisoners. Initially, no surgeon or religious minister was appointed to the hulk and, most difficult of all, there was no Code of Orders for maintaining authority and responsibility—very different from the situation on the Thames hulks, where Mollie Gillen convincingly argues that 'there was a considerable concern for the convict's physical and psychological welfare'.[19]

After the convicts had cut a hole in the deck of the *Dunkirk* and attempted to escape, Cowdry was desperate enough to approach the admiral at Plymouth. He was passed on to the Navy Board and then to Lord Sydney, who seemed less concerned with conditions on board than with the threat of escape. Finally, John Bastard, the MP for Devonshire wrote to Lord Sydney in early November 1784:

> The most serious consequences are daily to be apprehended from the want of a proper Code of Orders to regulate the Guard that is appointed to do the Duty on Board, as at present they are under no Control whatever either Civil or Military. The Consequence of which is, that the most atrocious as well as the most licentious Acts are committed on board not only by the Prisoners, but also by the Soldiery many of whom are nearly connected, if not old Accomplices with the Convicts...many of the prisoners are nearly if not quite naked.[20]

A short Code of Orders soon followed and the hulk 'fitted in a proper manner with different Cells and Hospitals, and the men and women kept separate'.[21] At the beginning of December the prisoners were belatedly issued with clothing: Hudson, Grace and the other male convicts received two shirts, one pair of stockings, one jacket, one pair of trousers, one cap and a pair of shoes.[22] Both boys signed for their clothing allowance with an X. Later that same month it seemed that the sentence of transportation would soon be effected. On 29 December the admiralty wrote to the Mayor of Plymouth in confidence: 'circumstances have...changed with respect to the removal or detention of the convicts on board the *Dunkirk*...It is at last determined that they shall forthwith be removed, with some others...to the coast of Africa.'[23] Such a plan failed to eventuate.

Life on board the hulk for John Hudson and his companions must have been a dreadful mixture of depravity and boredom. It is not clear if they were engaged in hard labour on the fortifications of Plymouth Harbour; perhaps their only regular (and rudimentary) duties were cooking and caring for the sick. Under Cowdry's determined and humane management, however, the prisoners' conditions improved. On the eve of his departure, with justification, Cowdry claimed that 'the Prisoners are now very healthy owing to the strict attentions that have been paid them'.[24] He prided himself on more than the physical well-being of his prisoners: "tis inconceivable the Fatigue I had and the Danger I went thro' with the Convicts before I could bring them to any kind of Order but now they will be easily managed if they are used properly'.[25] Considering that this was a mutinous group who had terrorised the countryside, Cowdry's achievement was worth a modest boast.

After March 1786 one of the few things recorded about John Hudson's daily life aboard the *Dunkirk* was his ration allowance, part of that distributed among groups of six prisoners:

> *Monday*—Eight pounds of Bread Sixteen Ounces to the Pound, two Pints and a half of Pease dressed into nearly Six Quarts of Soup for Dinner, three pints and an half of Oatmeal into the same Quantity of Bargoe for Supper with Salt each time.
>
> *Tuesday*—Four Pounds of Bread, four Pounds of Beef, Six Pounds of Potatoes Sixteen Ounces to the Pound, Six Quarts of Soup with an abundance of Vegetables Salt—Four pints of Oatmeal dressed into nearly Six Quarts of Bargoe for supper—But when Bullocks Heads were served them (which happened one day in a week upon an Average) Each Mess was served with half a Bullocks Head which was deemed equal to, and in lieu of four Pounds of Beef —
>
> *Wednesday*—The same as Monday—

Thursday—The same as Tuesday—
Friday—The same as Monday and Wednesday
Saturday and Sunday—The same as Tuesday and
Thursday—And an allowance of a Pint of Beer a day
to each Convict who chose to make use of the same.[26]

This ration was almost identical to that offered on the Thames
hulks at the same time. Any additional rations (fresh vegetables,
fruit, fish, milk) which might have diversified this stolid diet may
occasionally have been distributed through the largesse of friends
or philanthropically minded outsiders. The *Dunkirk*'s ration was
modelled on that given to the navy and was supposedly comparable in quality as well as quantity.

The sick prisoners on the *Dunkirk* were said to have received a
'comfortable allowance of Balm Tea, Sugar, Wine, Extra Oatmeal
for Gruel in addition to Medical Assistance'.[27] During part of John
Hudson's incarceration, Dr Richardson, the surgeon of the naval
hospital in Plymouth, was responsible for the health of prisoners
and wrote of their condition:

I have found them with almost every disease which
Vice and Immorality could produce. Some of them
had very bad venereal Complaints…some were over
whelmed with Dropsys, and others wasted by
Consumption, and those Disorders were aggravated by
long confinement in prison. And though it appeared
a Matter of surprise how people so contaminated
should recover at all, yet such were the effects of Air,
of cleanliness…and of diet, that though many were,
when first received into the ship through debility,
utterly unable to help themselves, yet they soon got
health and strength.

Had the Provisions been scanty, or of unwhole-
some quality, as had been erroneously set forth, the

Sick would not have soon recovered, and Fevers of a bad kind would have been generated, but few Died of Fevers, and taking all the circumstances together, I do not think that the mortality among the Convicts has been greater than among men of that description at other places. But whether this be the case, or not, sure I am that the utmost care was taken of them, and that none of the Convicts ever complained to me, either of the deficiency or ill quality of their provisions...[28]

This statement on conditions aboard the *Dunkirk* was produced in response to an official request following complaints from the convicts. The fulsome emphasis officials put on the quality of food, and the care lavished on their charges, cast them in the role of honest and highly considerate keepers. Whether conditions were ever so generous is uncertain. The *Dunkirk* appeared to be a healthy ship, for in the period March–December 1786 only six deaths were recorded. Yet even so, John Hudson's final removal to the First Fleet after two years on the *Dunkirk* would have been a welcome change of venue.

From the end of October 1786 women began arriving on the *Dunkirk* joining the twelve already there, including seven from the *Mercury*. After nearly three years on the hulk, Hudson was one of over 200 convicts, including forty-one women, sent on 10 March 1787 to the First Fleet for transportation to Australia. The *Dunkirk*'s prisoners were split between the *Friendship* and the *Charlotte* the following day and sailed for Portsmouth on 12 March. It was recorded that John Hudson behaved 'very well' and was thirteen years old.

Even on the eve of departure there was still a slim possibility of a reprieve, although this was unlikely for John because he had no-one to petition on his behalf. Nor did there seem to be any charities interested in young offenders which might have publicised his plight. The child was not as fortunate as the thief James Bartlett, who was delivered to a transport in January 1787 as a First Fleeter. In a remarkable reversal he was released with a free pardon following a petition from his wife and three children: 'On his industrious Labour [his wife] and tender family depend, and should he be transported, they must all inevitably be involved in Beggary, Misery, want and Ruin.'[29]

Had John Hudson's crime been committed a few years later than 1783 he might have avoided transportation altogether, and even found himself an object of charitable concern to the Philanthropic Society, founded in 1788:

> The Philanthropic Society aims at the prevention of crimes, by removing out of the way of evil counsel, and evil company, those children, who are, in the present state of things, destined to ruin…the children of convicts, or other infant poor who are engaged in vagrant or criminal courses.[30]

The corrupt natural family was here replaced by a moral, adoptive family. And in the Society's search for such children they certainly found cases which were remarkably similar to John Hudson's:

> A boy aged 13. Received sentence of death at the assizes at Nottingham, for a felony; was afterwards sent on board the hulks, to be transported to Botany Bay; but at length received his Majesty's most gracious pardon, on condition of his being received into the Philanthropic Reform.'[31]

The Society established workshops for boys under the direction of master workmen including printers, shoemakers, tailors, ropemakers, twine-spinners, carpenters and bricklayers. The girls were educated as 'menial servants' and employed within the Society 'in washing the linen, making their own cloathing, shirts for the boys,

&c'.[32] While no-one would deny that the Society assisted a hitherto ignored group, this assistance was extended only to a fraction of the needy.

Thousands of children were made orphans by the transportation of their single parent—usually a father—and a few were listed in the Society's publications:

> Thomas Burn, aged twelve—His father was a notorious thief, some time since transported to Botany Bay; his mother is in gaol for uttering counterfeit coin. The boy was connected with a gang of thieves, and has confessed a variety of atrocious acts; among others, he fired a blunderbuss, which he had just stolen, at a Watchman who had discharged his pistol at the boy as he was escaping over some out-houses...

> A girl aged 10, and her brother. The mother was transported to Botany Bay. Before she left England, these poor unfortunate children were wandering about, a prey to hunger and misery; her husband being dead, and having no friend to snatch them from impending ruin...

> A boy aged 8. His father, then confined in Newgate, was one of the miserable convicts who made their escape from Botany Bay, in a open boat; in which situation they remained ten days without food, and were brought to England in a Dutch vessel.[33]

Once John Hudson boarded the First Fleet he became, like so many of the convicts, lost to individual view. After being listed in the ship's muster he received no further mention at all. Could we assume from this silence that he caused no trouble on board, that his health remained stable and that he had no accidents? It would be three years before his name surfaced again, in a single line which records his punishment at Norfolk Island. After that he fades into silence. We may never learn what became of him. Did he marry, father children, receive a land grant or succumb to an early and unrecorded death?

There is another remarkable story which unfolded at the same time that John Hudson underwent his imprisonment and trial, his days on a hulk and his unwitting involvement in a convict mutiny. This tale is not a coda to Hudson's, but an interesting parallel. John Hudson's criminal actions ensured his berth on the First Fleet, but there were also innocent children caught up in this extraordinary voyage.

A CELEBRATED
FIRST FLEET FAMILY

The convicts' 'constant language was an apprehension of the impracticability of returning
home, the dread of a sickly passage, and the
fearful prospect of a distant and barbarous
country'.

Watkin Tench, 1789

HOW could the voices of children be heard above the clamour of
any embarkation? How could they compete with the swearing
of the crew, the barked orders mocked by the strident cry of the
seagulls, the wharfside confusion, the braying of animals as they
were loaded and the rattle of chains? Amidst such a cacophony
any gentler sound, like that of children's voices, had little hope of
being heard.

This was another stage in the lives of those dispossessed, not just
of freedom and of dignity, but of their very claim to common
humanity. These children of the First Fleet shared the same fate and
conditions as the convict parents they accompanied. They travelled
with their mothers on carts or wagons from all over England to
embarkation points, and the exodus continued from January 1787
until the day of sailing, 13 May 1787.

Among the first contingent, a large group of women from

Newgate Prison who were sent to the *Lady Penrhyn* on 6 January 1787, there was one child: Jane Jones arrived on board with her convict mother. This child's position of pre-eminence, if that is what it could be called, was short-lived. Within three days other children who had been Jones' companions in Newgate arrived on the same transport. On 11 March, four children with convict mothers arrived from the *Dunkirk* for embarkation on other vessels. These four had been part of the large-scale transfers from country gaols to the *Dunkirk* at the end of 1786 and had been kept on board the hulk for up to four months.

The familiar pattern of birth and death soon reasserted itself. After surviving the rigours of Newgate Prison, Hugh Sandlin and William Green, two male children of convict parents, died before the First Fleet sailed. If we look beyond the appalling conditions and a facile labelling of these mothers as undifferentiated whores, however, we find a remarkable range of convict women. These women chose not to abandon their children and leave them destitute. There is evidence of their efforts to maintain a family life. There is also, somewhat surprisingly, evidence that romance flourished in these dreadful conditions.

The foremost example of this is surely that of the convicts Henry Kable and Susannah Holmes and their child Henry, who was conceived and born in Norwich Castle Gaol. In the 1780s their story of youth, romance, separation and reconciliation elicited sympathy and interest from a broad range of the British public. It provided a rare corrective to the more common story of convict crime and immorality. The infant Henry Kable jnr, is the most celebrated example of an innocent child whose place on the First Fleet was not secured through his own actions, but by the decision of his convict parents.

The Kable story, as narrated in the English newspapers and magazines of the day, was remarkable for the sentiment it infused into two criminal lives. There was an open appeal to sympathy based on the unnatural separation of a mother from an unweaned child five months old. This was further bolstered by the separation of mother and father from each other, the rending apart of a young and helpless family. Then there was the affecting cliche of a gaoler with a heart of gold. All this was conveyed in a report published by *Scot's Magazine*, which was couched in highly emotive language. A saga of love blossoming in the most unlikely and least romantic situation. Of family values burgeoning where profligacy had formerly flourished:

November 1786

NARRATIVE RELATING TO A CONVICT ORDERED TO BE TRANSPORTED TO BOTANY BAY

In consequence of the late determination of government to send some convicts to Botany Bay, with a design of establishing a colony in New South Wales, an order lately came down to the keeper of Norwich Gaol to send such female convicts as were then in prison to Plymouth, to be in readiness to go upon that expedition. Three unhappy women, who had been a long while in the castle under sentence of transportation, were accordingly sent, and were committed to the care of Mr Simpson, turnkey of the prison.[1]

One of these unfortunate females was the mother of an infant about five months old, a very fine babe, whom she had suckled from its birth. The father of the child was likewise a felon under similar sentence, and had been in prison more than three years. He had repeatedly expressed a wish to be married to this woman, and though seldom permitted to see the child, he discovered a remarkable fondness for it: and that the mother's only comfort was derived from its smiles, was evident from her particularly tender manner nursing it.

When the order came down for her removal, the man was much distressed, and very importunate to attend the woman, and application was made to the minister to permit him to go; but so many similar applications having been made, this could not be complied with. The miserable woman was therefore obliged to go without the man, who offered to be her husband, that he might be her companion and protector during a long and melancholy voyage, and in a distant and unknown land. The child, however, was still her property, as the laws of England, which are distinguished by the spirit of humanity which framed them, forbid so cruel an act as that of separating an infant from its mother's breast.

When Mr Simpson arrived at Plymouth with his party, he found that they were to be put on board a hulk, which lies there till the ship which goes to the South Sea is ready to take them.[2] He therefore took a boat, and went to the vessel to deliver up his prisoners. Some forms, which the gaoler of Norwich had not been apprised of, having been omitted, the Captain of the hulk at first refused to take them, and these miserable creatures were kept three hours in an open boat, before they were received into their new abode of wretchedness. And when they were admitted, the Captain, finding that one of them had an infant, peremptorily refused to take it on board, saying, that he had no orders to take children; neither the intreaties of Mr Simpson, nor the agonies of the poor wretch, could prevail upon the Captain even to permit the babe to remain until instructions could be received from the minister.[3] Simpson was therefore obliged to take the child; and the frantic mother was led to her cell, execrating the cruelty of the man under whose care she was now placed, and vowing to put an end to her life as soon as she could obtain the means. Shocked at the nonparalleled brutality of the Captain, and his humanity not less affected by the agonies of the poor woman, and the situation of the helpless babe, Mr Simpson resolved still, if possible, to get it restored to her.

No way was left but an immediate personal application to Lord Sydney; and having once before been with his Lordship on a business of humanity, he was encouraged to hope that he should succeed, could he but have an interview with him. He therefore immediately went back to Plymouth, and set off in the first coach to London, carrying the child all the way on his knee, and feeding it at the different inns he arrived at as well as he could.

When he came to London, he placed the child with a careful woman, and instantly posted to Lord Sydney's. Neither his Lordship nor his secretary were to be spoken to, at least this was told him when he addressed the person in waiting at the office: but humanity will not be restrained by forms; acting under the influence of a superior power, it moves forward, unchecked by the fear of offending any earthly one. Mr Simpson was denied admittance, but in vain; for he pressed forward into one of the offices, and told his story to one of the secretaries, who attended very properly to it, and promised to do all in his power to promote the object of his humane petition, but feared it would be impossible for him to see Lord Sydney for several days; he begged, however, of his gentleman to prepare an order for the restoration of the child, and determined to await in the hall for the chance of seeing his Lordship pass, that he might prevail on him to sign it.

Fortunately, not long after, he saw Lord Sydney descend the stairs; he instantly ran to him; his Lordship very naturally shewed an unwillingness at first to attend to an application made to him in so strange and abrupt a manner, but Mr Simpson immediately related the reason of his intrusion, and described, as he felt, the exquisite misery he had lately been witness to, expressing his fears, lest, in the instant he was pleading for her, the unhappy woman, in the wildness of her despair, should have deprived herself of existence. Lord Sydney was greatly affected, and paid much attention to the particular circumstances of his narration, and instantly promised that the child should be restored, commending, at the same time, Mr Simpson's spirit and humanity. Encouraged by this, he made a further appeal to his Lordship's humanity in behalf of the father of the child, which proved equally successful; for his Lordship ordered that he likewise should be sent to Plymouth to accompany the child and its mother, directing at the same time, that they should be married before they went on board, and adding, that he himself would pay the fees.[4]

One of his Lordship's secretaries wrote immediately

to Plymouth, that the woman might be informed of the success of Mr Simpson's application; and he, after visiting the child, and giving directions that it might be taken care of in his absence, set off for Norwich, and communicated the glad tidings to the unhappy father of the child. The poor man, who is a fine healthy young fellow, seemed very grateful to Lord Sydney and to Mr Simpson, and was made very happy by this change of circumstances; and it is to be hoped that he may, notwithstanding his past situation, turn out a useful individual of the new community. He set off for Plymouth, accompanied by Mr Simpson, who, after the fatigues, anxieties, and vexations of his first journey, to that place, having travelled, three days and nights without sleep, no doubt will be amply recompensed by the satisfaction he must experience, in thus having been the means of rescuing two unhappy people from a situation of distress scarcely to be equalled.[5]

It is proper to observe, that Captain Phillips [sic], who is to go out with the convicts to Botany Bay, is a man of very different disposition to the person alluded to in this narrative; but he, unfortunately, had no power to interfere.

The conclusion of the above relation cannot be more properly given, than in the words of Mr Simpson himself, who wrote the following letter a few days ago to a gentleman in Bath:

Dear Sir,

It is with the utmost pleasure that I inform you of my safe arrival with my little charge at Plymouth: but it would take an abler pen than mine to describe the joy that the mother received her infant and her intended husband with. Suffice it to say, that their transports, that the tears that flowed from their eyes, with the innocent smiles of the babe, on the sight of the mother, who had saved her milk for it, drew tears likewise from my eyes; and it was with the utmost regret that I parted with the child, after having travelled with it on my lap for upwards of 700 miles backwards and forwards. But the blessings I received at the different inns on the road have amply repaid me.

I am, with great respect, your humble servant.

John Simpson
Plymouth Nov. 16 [6]

This touching story was well calculated to arouse the sympathy of the reading public and its plaintive appeal to noble sentiment encouraged them to donate £20—about twice the annual salary of a labourer at the time.[7] The money was used to purchase books, clothes and some comforts for the young family.

After persistent coverage in London and provincial newspapers and magazines, the story was reprinted in 1787 as a twelve-page epilogue to Daniel Defoe's popular *Voyage Round the World*.[8] The year after that, the young couple's story was the subject of a letter from Port Jackson to the under secretary of the Navy Board.[9] And then in 1789 a London newspaper published a letter from Henry Kable to this mother.[10] What was it about the Kable family's story which so aroused public interest?

The answer lies in the power and influence of the mass media to conjure a nine-day national wonder from a regional *cause célèbre*. In this story the popular press replaced stereotypes of hardened criminals, heartless gaolers and aloof officials with their diametric opposites. The venality, corruption and brutality of eighteenth-century prison life were replaced with an example of compassion and selflessness. The press rewrote the crime into a touching family tragedy rather than an impersonal problem contributing only to a tally of alarming statistics.

Much of the interest centred around Mr Simpson, whose efforts were more than noble and rendered him a hero of the day. His victory in reuniting the family on the First Fleet enabled readers to respond with sentimental empathy. In ten days this turnkey travelled over the makeshift and dangerous roads of late eighteenth-century England from Norwich to Plymouth to London, to Norwich and back to Plymouth. For one leg of that journey he nursed an unweaned infant, procured its sustenance, bravely stood his ground in London and gained an audience with the Home Secretary. Such actions belied the idea that all officials were uncaring and unsympathetic to the anguish of convict separation.

Equally newsworthy were the convict parents. Neither Henry Kable nor Susannah Holmes was a notorious murderer, celebrated pickpocket or prominent rogue. Furthermore, neither knew public figures who could petition on their behalf or would be interested in keeping their case in the public eye. The reason for the pair's unique and continued profile was the affecting fate of the young child at the centre of the whole affair: a young innocent caught up his parents' fate and transported to the opposite side of the world. Surely this was the distinguishing feature which captured public attention and sentiment? Indeed, for many in this audience, this may have been the first time that they realised that infants were part of the human cargo of the First Fleet.

Today, the story affords us a late eighteenth-century example of public compassion and official sympathy. One of the very first newspaper reports of the event elevated official solicitude, penal tolerance and public humanity into national virtues: 'when the object is humanity, and delay would materially affect the happiness of even the meanest subject in the kingdom, the Minister himself not only attends to complaints properly addressed, but promptly and effectively affords relief'.[11]

The characters in this saga enjoyed a brief celebrity because they were recast: instead of conforming to the stereotypes of hardened and repugnant criminals they were re-created in the press of the day as 'unfortunate' and 'distressed' with a remarkable 'fondness' for and 'tender manner' towards their infant. Through journalistic hyperbole their dilemma became a 'situation of distress scarcely to be equalled'.

The truth may be more complicated as well as less romantic than the much retold version. Impassioned petitions from the chairman of the Quarter Sessions to Lord Sheffield and thence to Lord Sydney had been dispatched within days of the order for Susannah's removal to the hulk. In a neat reversal of culpability these petitions claimed that the two convicts 'never were confederate in any Crime or Misdemeanour, but that of Child making'.[12]

Regardless of where and when official intervention and sympathy occurred, their crime of housebreaking and burglary was replaced by a crime of society against nature. When the two convicts were turned into a young swain and his sweetheart, the crime became society's, in its separation of them and its disregard for the natural felicity of familial bonds. It was a remarkable reversal and an effective piece of propaganda—guaranteed to appeal to a public where charitable and philanthropic gestures were becoming a fashionable exercise.

Since the 1760s the cult of sensibility had eagerly begun to embrace new touchstones for a developing social conscience. Writers of the day expressed their concern for prisoners, children, animals, slaves, chimneysweeps and the insane in their novels, plays, magazines, songs and pamphlets. The public was literally reading itself into a new role. Sentiment replaced cynicism and the domestic virtues of the Georgian middle class became a national ideal.

Sensibility was perceived to be a modern quality, an achievement of the civilising process and a hallmark of the late eighteenth century. But sensibility that luxuriated in emotion was socially irresponsible—appropriate charitable positions were increasingly sought and embraced. The plight of the Kable family was a heaven-sent opportunity for a widespread display of such sensibility. By combining so many appealing elements—an emerging esteem for motherhood, a sentimental view of children, interest in prison reform, the topical interest in the First Fleet and the frisson of a romance growing in the most adverse conditions—the story provided an occasion for a national display and outpouring of sensibility. And, above all, the late eighteenth century loved a fine gesture. Here was real life imitating fiction.

Although *The Times* felt that the tale was 'exaggerated in the detail' and was contrived 'to feel the pulse of public credulity', the extent to which liberties may have been taken with the facts of the story is largely irrelevant.[13] When the anonymous sufferings of First Fleet convicts were replaced by a specific case of distress, the public responded with humanitarian concern.

Of all the children of convicts on the First Fleet, Henry Kable jnr was the most fortunate. Against all odds he accompanied both parents into exile, became part of a stable family unit in a penal colony and later enjoyed a life of opportunity and advantage. Transportation in his case may have been a blessing. Surely the Kable family could never have experienced such a reversal of fortune had they remained in England?

A FLOATING NURSERY

AN infants' nursery, a farmyard and a menagerie. When the First Fleet sailed on 13 May 1787 it was all of these things as much as it was a floating gaol. Additional livestock was taken aboard at each port of call and animal and human births continued until George Worgan, a Fleet surgeon on the *Sirius* was reminded of a biblical parallel: 'each Ship like another Noah's Ark'. By the end of the voyage the Fleet had carried Captain Phillip's greyhounds and horses and the Reverend Johnson's kittens as well as a motley combination of sheep, cattle, pigs, goats, turkeys, geese, ducks, chickens, rabbits, pigeons and dogs—and nineteen newborn children.

Priority was not given to the human cargo: at the Cape of Good Hope women and children were dispossessed of the home they had known for the previous six months and transferred from the *Friendship* to other ships—to make room for an additional intake of sheep. The chief surgeon on the *Lady Penrhyn*, Arthur

Bowes Smyth, seemed as concerned with the health of this diverse animal population as with recording human births and deaths. In a laconic entry for 31 May 1787 he gave equal attention to goats and infants: 'Mr. Watt's Goat had 2 Kids, a male & female. At 3 O'Clock p.m. Isabella Lawson one of the Convicts was deliver'd of a Girl.'[1]

Few of the animals survived the voyage—most were eaten, died or were washed overboard. The human mortality rate was much lower, and an examination of the medical preparedness and attention offered on the Fleet dispels many misconceptions about convict treatment in 1787.

For many of the convicts who had spent years in prison or on a hulk, the Fleet offered unprecedented medical care, regular meals and a more salubrious environment above and below decks. All of the six convict transports carried a surgeon, and Bowes Smyth reported at length on convict health and wellbeing:

> It is pretty extraordinary how very healthy the Convicts…in general have been, during so long a passage & where there was a necessity to stowg. them so thick together…few Marines going out of England upon Service were ever so amply provided for as these Convicts are, & the Surgeons & Officers of the different Ships pay such strict attention to their keeping themselves & their Births [berths] well air'd & perfectly clean…[2]

The health record did in fact vary from ship to ship and, as far as mishaps were concerned, the women were particularly vulnerable. Jane Bonner was one victim of this precarious shipboard existence. She suffered a violent blow on the head from a jolly-boat which came loose in rough weather and died a week later. Phoebe Norton fell overboard but was rescued. Mary Davis fell down the ship's hatchway and although 'pitched on her head' received no material injury, while Margaret Bunn suffered a badly scalded leg.[3]

Those most at risk at sea were pregnant women, nursing mothers and their newborn babies, crawling infants and young children. They had to contend with the daily hazards of life aboard a pitching ship buffeted by wind, sea and rain, living in cramped conditions where it was often impossible to stand upright below decks and with stairs and passageways slippery with water and animal refuse. There was also the darkness of a ship's hold where candles and lanterns had to be carefully guarded to prevent accidents. Yet in spite of all this danger the women and children seemed remarkably safe.

William Abel, Jane Davis and Edward Dwan had been born on board before the Fleet sailed and there were nineteen births on the voyage out. No woman died during labour, six had stillbirths and only three children died at sea—this total excludes Hugh Sandlin and William Green who died before the Fleet sailed. Compared with the incidence of death in childbirth and the infant mortality rate back in England, the Fleet offered a commendable chance of survival.

The emerging popularity of textbooks such as William Buchan's *Domestic Medicine* does not necessarily mean that guides to childbirth and infant management indicated actual, and not merely medically preferred, practices. But while it must be admitted that many of Buchan's recommendations could not have reached the mass of the uneducated population in a direct way, it would be a mistake to assume that this text only influenced the middle class. Women from the lower classes may have had contact with advances in childbirth and child care in at least four highly effective if indirect ways.

They may have been introduced to some of the advances via the charitable visits of informed women into their homes. Furthermore, the thinking of more enlightened households may have filtered down through their domestic staff and into the wider community. A prime example of this influence from above was the delivery of Queen Charlotte's last child in 1783, which was attended by a male midwife, Dr James Ford, and was nationally publicised.

More formally, there was the influence of the Dispensary for the Infant Poor, lying-in hospitals and the Royal Maternity Charity, all established from the mid-century specifically for the lower classes. These organisations also encouraged an experimental basis in the emerging field of obstetrics and trained a new generation of nurses and midwives (male and female) who then disseminated new methods and practices. In 1783 Dr George Armstrong claimed that a decade of work in the Dispensary for the Infant Poor was sufficient time to introduce substantial change:

> Cleanliness amongst the parents, nurses, and children, I encourage and commend…and whenever any of them has come dirty to the Dispensary…I have constantly reproved them for it; in consequence of which it has very seldom lately happened that any one came who was not clean and decently dressed.[4]

Armstrong had a further interesting observation as to the broader spread of the Dispensary's influence:

> As persons in the lower stations of life have a more free intercourse and communication with one another, than those of a higher rank, and make their children a more frequent topic of conversation, for want of other subjects…it is natural to imagine, that by means of this charity the above-mentioned instructions are now become generally known and observed by the Industrious Poor in and about London.[5]

Was Dr Armstrong suggesting that worthwhile change could start with the lower classes, or that their example was something to emulate? Other writers certainly were lauding practices among the poor, with the lower-class habits of breastfeeding, of infant clothing, and simple infant diet and exercise being promoted to middle- and upper-class readers.

In the same decade efforts were made to spread a vision of bourgeois family harmony as seen in Sarah Trimmer's popular work of the time, *The Oeconomy of Charity*:

> By observing the almost universal success of poor women in suckling their own children, and the satisfaction usually attending it, young ladies would be prepossessed in favour of this duty…as the bond of reciprocal affection, the cement of family concord.[6]

William Cadogan's notes on child-rearing in the different classes provided an alarming contrast:

> The Mother who has only a few Rags to cover her Child loosely, and little more than her own Breast to feed it, sees it healthy and strong, and very soon able to shift for itself; while the puny Insect, the Heir and Hope of a rich Family lies languishing under a Load of Finery, that overpowers his limbs, abhorring and rejecting the Dainties he is crammed with, till he dies a Victim to the mistaken Care and Tenderness of his fond Mother.[7]

Those who formerly had been credited with establishing standards were now urged to look to the lower classes as an example. By the late 1780s when the First Fleet sailed, it was likely that this pattern of thinking informed the medical treatment and advice given to pregnant women and mothers aboard.

Earlier in the century pregnancy was treated as an abnormal condition. The fact that women stopped menstruating during

pregnancy was seen as a medical problem insofar as it left them
without a regular purgative cycle.[8] Before the 1750s the care of
infants was left to old women, nurses and midwives. Even after
surgeons (exclusively male) began to annex this new medical
territory to their own, George Armstrong, one of the first
children's specialists in London, reported in 1783 that many were
'not fond of practising among infants...[and] make no scruple to
assert that there is nothing to be done for children when they are
ill.'[9] Armstrong further remarked that: 'Children while in their
infancy, especially if the young family is numerous, and the parents
in straitened circumstances, are not thought of sufficient
consequence to be much attended to, unless some sudden or
violent illness happens to give an alarm.'[10]

Cape Town Harbour, 13 October 1787. The Fleet arrived in the
early evening, five months after leaving England. To someone like
the convict Jane Langley, who was soon to give birth, this temporary landfall must have seemed an especially good omen. For
the following week she would have been grateful for the calm
anchorage of the harbour as well as the improved diet of fresh
beef, mutton, fruit and vegetables, bread and an increased
allowance of water. Once again, there was no favouritism with the
victualling: 'The troops, men, women, and children were served
with a pound and half of soft bread, and an equal quantity of beef
or mutton daily, and with wine in lieu of spirits. The convicts,
men, women, and children, had the same allowance as the troops,
except wine.'[11]

Jane Langley's first view of the town with its lofty mountain
backdrop was picturesque and an engaging respite from the
monotony of life at sea. Closer to shore, however, she was greeted
by a line of gallows and wheels 'for breaking Felons upon' with

several occupied 'by the mangled Bodies of the unhappy wretches who suffer'd upon them: their right hands...cut off & fixt by a large nail to the side of the Wheel'.[12] Such a sight could hardly be a salutary experience for anyone, let alone a woman about to go into labour. Surgeons and midwives would for once have been in agreement that the expectant mother should avoid all such uncomely sights and concentrate on beauty. And yet much in Langley's past nine months was the exact opposite of that recommended in the contemporary manuals of midwifery:

> Women when pregnant should lead a regular and temperate life carefully avoiding whatever is to disagree with the stomach; they should breathe a free open air; their company should be agreeable and cheerful; their exercise should be moderate, and adapted to their peculiar situation; they should...avoid crowds, confinement, every situation which renders them under any disagreeable restriction, agitation of body from violent or improper exercise...and whatever disturbs either the body or mind.[13]

Combined with Jane Langley's apprehension about the birth and her future in a convict colony was the added knowledge that she would be an unmarried mother, whose brief liaison with a sailor on her ship offered no promise of future co-habitation. Some modern historians claim that 'on the convict ships, evidence of pregnancy, far from being seen as requiring special concessions and care, became an overt statement about a woman's prior sexual activities, thus increasing both the scrutiny and the moral censure of the male officials'.[14] Could Jane Langley ever have imagined that her first born would become 'an exceedingly reputable woman' in New South Wales?[15] Lying on board the ship she could hardly have imagined her own long and stable marriage in the colony—a marriage to a marine that produced seven children. If that was her future, what about her past? Did she think back to her desperate life in London where such possibilities would have been highly unlikely?

It was in September 1785 that Jane Langley faced sentencing for theft in the Old Bailey. About twenty-one, she had served an apprenticeship as a tambour worker (embroiderer) and, like so many from her background, appeared to engage in casual prostitution. Court records describe her as tall with very curly hair and a dark complexion. Despite the best efforts of character witnesses, Langley was sentenced to seven years' transportation. She left Newgate Prison on 6 January 1787 to board the *Lady Penrhyn*. As part of the first group of women to board the Fleet she waited another four months before sailing.

Within that period there was much confusion, change and uncertainty. Authority and responsibilities were still being finalised and the situation of the women convicts was easily abused. It was not until April that the senior lieutenant on board issued orders to keep the women apart from the sailors. Two weeks after that order an incomplete roll call led to five women being found in the sailor's quarters. Perhaps Jane Langley was one of those whose 'desire...to be with the men was so uncontrollable that neither shame...nor fear of punishment, would deter them from making their way through the bulk heads to the apartments assigned the seamen'.[16] From similar reports on board the *Friendship* one imagines that these lascivious women raped the sailors. Whatever the case, Jane Langley was certainly pregnant before the Fleet sailed in mid-May.

What was it in the attitudes of the day that consistently represented these women as voracious sexual creatures, insatiable and predatory? The First Fleet journals are all written by men—there is no complementary female record. These accounts are by men whose class level and background immediately distance them from these women, although sexual need served to bridge this chasm and many liaisons were established, even before the Fleet sailed. Deeply ingrained misogyny and hypocrisy paints these women as men's playthings and yet at the same time attributes an over-whelming and grotesque sexuality to them. One of the major sexual myths of the day presented women as sexually insatiable creatures once their desires were aroused—an idea traceable in many contemporary medical handbooks and much eighteenth-century fiction.[17]

This idea, of course, was shocking as well as titillating to a male audience. Any woman whose sexual desires were not directed towards marriage and motherhood was labelled unnatural. In prison, on a hulk and on the First Fleet, sexual liaisons were almost always perfunctory and functional—an animal indulgence of sex without sensibility. In some eyes it was an unleashing of selfish passions with danger to the social order. Such unruly sexual behaviour produced illegitimate births, disrupted legal interests and subverted the accepted sexual roles. By the end of the eighteenth century Jane Langley and her companions were figures from an earlier age of sexual licence and depravity.

Two realms of experience and expertise in childbirth intersected on the *Lady Penrhyn*—the collective culture of women attendant at births and the emerging world of medicine. In the domain of female control and solidarity, childbirth and its ritual provided the most potent opportunity for these women to assert personal value; to be more than a convict. Childbirth was a great leveller and exposed all classes of women to the same risks.

In contrast, the world of eighteenth-century medical authority was exclusively male and had been steadily encroaching into the territory of midwifery all century. By 1780 the English aristocracy had abandoned the traditional female midwife for a male accoucheur, though this radical change was only slowly introduced in the lower levels of society.[18] There the traditional services of midwives, female family members and neighbouring mothers were maintained and a surgeon was only called in when some difficulty arose. The belief that midwives were unskilled, ignorant and often traded on the superstitions of their clients is today considered to owe as much to medical disdain as to historical accuracy: in 1769 Buchan's text for household use warned against 'the ridiculous custom which still prevails in some country-places, of collecting a number of women together upon such occasions'.[19] These women were judged to 'crowd the house...obstruct the necessary attendants...hurt the patient with the noise and by their untimely and impertinent advice, do much mischief'.[20]

Jane Langley's delivery was one of about twenty-five such events on the Fleet, including miscarriages and stillbirths. Yet among all the exhaustive preparations for outfitting the voyage there was, not surprisingly, no evidence of a woman's touch. Victualling for children was initially overlooked, no midwives or matrons were appointed, women's and children's clothing was in short supply or forgotten, cloths for menstruation, birthing and antenatal care were not even considered. There seemed to be no awareness during these preparations that women and children needed special treatment with food, personal hygiene and medical supplies. When John White, chief surgeon of the First Fleet, made out his first shopping list from the colony for medical supplies he concluded with a request for '6 pair old Sheets'.[21]

The Second Fleet, which arrived two years later, fared better, and Lord Sydney wrote to the Treasury in April 1789 specifically requesting supplies for the pregnant women:

> Several of the Female Convicts embarked on board
> the *Juliana*, who are pregnant, are represented to be

destitute of any of those Supplies which are requisite for the Care of their Infants after their Birth. I cannot therefore omit to recommend it to your Lordships to order a small supply of Linen and Flannel to be put on board for these purposes, together with a proportion of Soap which I am persuaded is equally essential and necessary.[22]

This consideration was later extended to another ship in the Second Fleet which was also loaded with quantities of linen and flannel.[23] Such an omission on the First Fleet turned the women into scavengers—Langley and her companions were, in the words of Bowes Smyth, reduced to 'plundering the sailors...of their necessary cloaths & cutting them up for some purpose of their own'.[24]

The conditions under which pregnant women made the voyage and gave birth do not appear to have been an issue of concern to the authorities. In 1802 Sir John Fitzpatrick wrote:

no one matter...so soon contaminates the air in a crowded place, and a hot climate as the unavoidable consequences of women's lying in where they cannot have the necessary means of cleanliness or fresh air and where they must be subject to every inconvenience arising from the crowd and clatter of all about them.[25]

In the surgeons' logs from the First Fleet, there is no detailed description of childbirth at sea, and sometimes not even a reliable record of deliveries. To construct some idea of the event we must turn to medical and midwifery texts of the day for contemporary attitudes and practices.

Jane Langley was in Cape Town harbour for just over one week before going into labour. While there was no formal lying-in chamber, surely there was a more private area away from the communal living quarters for her confinement? Personal space, for everyone on board, was presumably limited. As soon as the pains came on, all the knots, laces and fastenings of Langley's clothes were undone. With the premium on linen and flannel, Langley was likely forced to deliver her child upon straw, which was freely available. Two fellow convicts on board, Ann Colpitts and Sarah Burdo, possibly took the place of an official midwife—they later established names for themselves in this calling. In contrast, it has been claimed that the Second Fleet included a small coterie of free women (convicts' wives or de factos) given passage by the government in order to practice midwifery on board and in the colony.[26]

There is no doubt Jane Langley was fortunate to have been on board the *Lady Penrhyn*. This was the vessel which was judged 'the most healthy ship in the Fleet' and had more medical staff than any other: Surgeon Arthur Bowes Smyth was assigned to care for the women, together with two assistants.[27]

Even with a birth imminent it was unlikely that everyone in attendance washed their hands. Adequate ventilation, scrupulous cleanliness on the part of all attendants as well as of towels, bed linen and instruments were hardly common practice. One of Langley's companions might have applied a lubricant to stretch the ligaments and soften the tissues. Among the upper classes in Britain at the time the favoured position for delivery was lying on a bed on the left side, with the knees drawn up towards the abdomen. This position, though convenient for the attendant and certainly more 'modest' than others, occasioned a projection of the child in a line unfavourable to the perineum. The medical opinion at the time recommended a position that had the woman on her hands and knees. This was advocated in 1782 as 'a position instinctively fought for, and often, recommended in cases of difficulty and distress'.[28]

If this was a normal delivery with everything proceeding correctly—the situation of the baby, the position of the uterus and the progress of the labour—then most of the assistance came from the women attending. Once the child was delivered it was laid on its side, with its back to the mother and at a little distance from her, to prevent any accident from a gush of blood or water. Then, when the child cried, breathed freely or otherwise displayed signs of life, the cord was tied and divided. Within half an hour the placenta was expelled and thrown overboard. The baby was then washed and checked for any deformities. If, however, a birth did present problems, the surgeon intervened and likely resorted to using his metal midwifery instruments: crotchets, knives, fillets, speculum matrices, forceps, pincers and the vectis. There was still a deep-seated fear of the surgeon, who relied on these tools rather than the manual approach of midwives.

Was Jane Langley given any drug from the surgeon's pharmacy to alleviate her pain? An accepted belief of the time, as stated in a midwifery manual, was that women like Langley from the lower classes did not feel the pain of childbirth to the same extent as their upper-class sisters. Because of their 'less exquisite feel-ings…the lower class of women have more easy and favourable births, than those who live in affluence'.[29] And because of these 'less exquisite feelings', women from the lower classes endured more robust manual treatment during childbirth. Delicacy of treatment and the niceties of modest and indulgent attendance were all bought for a fee.

After the delivery, Langley would have been swathed, but not too tightly. In 1781 the professor of Midwifery from Edinburgh University, Alexander Hamilton, advised that 'the belly should be made moderately firm, by the application of a table napkin, folded like a compress, and secured by pinning the broad bands of the skirt or petticoat over it'.[30] However cursory Langley's treatment during childbirth may seem, she was probably given the same attention she would have received in England. Were there any little comforts for her once the labour was completed? Was she given cinnamon water or bread dipped in cold wine; was an opium pill or five drops of laudanum administered to her?

As late as 1786, *Chamber's Cyclopaedia* still advocated warmth, sweating, a darkened room and nine days' bed-rest after labour. Jane Langley was in no position to be indulged with such luxuries, and mother and child would have soon been absorbed back into the routine of shipboard life.

Soon after birth the baby would have been introduced to the breast. By the middle of the eighteenth century a proliferation of medical handbooks focused on the issue of breastfeeding. Although not all writers agreed about the traditional value of midwives or the propriety of men taking over this role, they were united in one thing: the desirability of breastfeeding by the mother. The colour and consistency of a mother's first milk, so different from later breast milk, was regarded by many as highly undesirable for the infant and was usually expressed and discarded before the child was given suck. The baby was thus denied the highly nutritional and immunological benefits from colostrum. From the mid-eighteenth century, however, mothers were urged to breastfeed within twenty-four hours of delivery instead of waiting three or four days for normal-looking milk to appear.

Another radical change in late eighteenth-century attitudes was that motherhood began to be seen as sanctifying women. In 1753, in one of the earliest writings in this line, James Nelson's *An Essay on the Government of Children* combined moral and medical imperatives:

> Mothers by suckling their Children cherish that Tenderness which Nature has implanted in them towards their Offspring. For Experience shews, that

the Office of suckling considerably augments in them the Affection from whence that Tenderness flows; serves as Fuel to keep their fond Breasts in one perpetual Glow; and by sweetening their Care, enables them likewise to bring the tender Infants thro' their helpless Age...All Mothers who have experienc'd it, whose Minds are temper'd with natural Affection, assure us, that there is an inexpressible Pleasure in giving Suck.[31]

By 1784 the advocacy became more medically based: 'not only is the breast-milk the only natural, and proper food for infants, but suckling also conduces to the easy recovery of the mother'.[32]

When Langley suckled her newborn child she simply continued the practice of someone from her class. A century earlier it was common for mothers to withhold breastfeeding for up to one month after delivery and administer a variety of purges. This practice often resulted in milk fever, when the milk stagnated in the breast and encouraged infection and abscesses. Experiments from the middle of the eighteenth century in lying-in hospitals promoted a new understanding that breastfeeding from the first day protected mothers from contracting this fever. Since the lying-in hospitals and the Royal Maternity Charity catered for respectable poor women, 'it was the poor rather than the richer women in society who were subjected to this change in medical ideas and thus first benefited from them'.[33]

Whatever her mixed emotions, Jane Langley's successful delivery was something to be celebrated. One ceremony not neglected on the First Fleet was the christening. *The Book of Common Prayer* required that a child be baptised on the first or second Sunday after birth. In practice, whether on land or aboard a convict ship, some leeway occurred. An unidentified officer writing days after Langley's delivery described a group christening of convicts' children as an event of 'Great glee' with 'an additional allowance of grog being distributed to the crews of those ships where births took place'.[34] Langley's daughter was christened Henrietta Skirving on 4 November 1787. Even today the child's paternity remains uncertain, though it is thought the father was the seaman Philip Scriven.

The 1780s were something of a turning point, when better sanitation and improved obstetrics began to make childbirth less dangerous and less of a trauma to mother and child. Popular opinion slowly started to discard centuries of tenacious and ill-founded habits, replacing them with professional care and advice. Jane Langley and others who gave birth on the First Fleet were among a new generation of mothers who received the direct benefits of these new attitudes towards childbirth.

VOYAGE AND LANDFALL

ELIZABETH Hayward was the youngest of the women convicts, listed as a thirteen year old, when delivered to the *Lady Penrhyn* on 22 January 1787. She had stolen clothes valued at seven shillings from the man to whom she was apprenticed on 19 December 1786. Her loot was later traced to a pawnshop—a naive attempt at robbery that was doomed to be discovered.

Elizabeth received no mercy from her master although he must have known that he consigned her to a harsh and dangerous fate. What was Newgate like for this child prisoner in 1786? This was thirty years before Elizabeth Fry began her philanthropic work for women prisoners which changed 'drunkenness to sobriety...riot to order...clamour to quietness...obscenity to decency'.[1] In 1786 the most vivid public image of the women of Newgate was of them begging through the bars, importuning passers-by with vociferous cursing and obscene exhortations. A sheriff of the City of London described the women's situation at the prison in 1808:

> Among the women, all the ordinary feelings of the sex
> are outraged by their indiscriminate association. The
> shameless victims of lust and profligacy are placed in
> the same chamber with others who...still preserve
> their respect for decency and decorum.[2]

If this radical change in Elizabeth Hayward's world was not
enough, consider just how abrupt these changes were: she committed her crime a week before Christmas, was taken to Newgate and
sentenced at the Old Bailey on 12 January 1787 to seven years'
transportation, and less than two weeks later was on board the
Lady Penrhyn.

She would be there for one full month before Arthur Bowes
Smyth, the major chronicler of the vessel's voyage, arrived. He was
originally appointed as surgeon to the ship's company, but soon
after the voyage began John Altree, who was assigned to care for
the convicts fell ill and Bowes Smyth replaced him. The quality of
the new surgeon's caring and the value of Governor Phillip's
choice are evident in the remarkable health record achieved on
board this transport.

Although the *Lady Penrhyn* carried more than 100 women, all
except one of those originally consigned survived the eight-and-
a-half-month voyage. The one fatality was Elizabeth Beckford,
whose age was given variously as seventy and eighty-two and who
had been ill before the ship left England. Another death, that of
Jane Parkinson, occurred less than a month after her transferral
from the *Friendship* to the *Lady Penrhyn* at the Cape of Good Hope.
Mary Lawson was the only child to die on the ship during the long
voyage.

Even before the Fleet sailed women on board the *Lady Penrhyn*
were reported as being 'very sick with the motion of the Ship'.[3]
One convict, Elizabeth Bruce, fell from the forecastle and broke
her right leg while the ship was still in port. Once the voyage

began, another would fall and break her ribs.[4] One imagines that few women endured the long voyage without some injury. Bowes Smyth wrote that 'Many of the women…received hurts & bruises from falls' and many 'were wash'd out of their Births [berths] by the Seas we ship'd'.[5]

Apart from physical dangers, the women were also beset with the anguish of separation from home and family—a separation with no possibility of a reunion. An 1830s account from Dr Thrasycles Clarke on the female convict ship *Kains* describes this anguish, and gives a voice to these women whose words of suffering will never be known. A woman was 'fretting about some of her Children which she had left behind in England [and] when the wind blows a little harder than ordinary she then becomes so alarmed that she can neither sleep nor remain in bed but is wandering about the Prison in a state of the greatest trepidation'.[6]

The physical dangers and psychological anguish of this new world were matched by an equal weight of moral danger. Remember that, before the Fleet sailed, an unexpected roll call on the night of 19 April 1787 revealed five of Elizabeth Hayward's fellow-prisoners in the crew's quarters. There was an attitude that the women were most at fault for this transgression, and it was they who were put in irons. The sexual tension one can observe from such incidents was a catalyst for further unrest on the First Fleet voyage.

Why were the middle-class officers and the ships' surgeons so shocked by these women in their attempt to contest some social space? Even by late Georgian standards and certainly before the Victorian idealisation of motherhood and family emerged, these convict women challenged the traditional view of femininity. They were a threat to more than just the law. Their subversive behaviour undermined the social order; their sexual autonomy produced social chaos. Dr Clarke wrote:

If there ever was a hell afloat it must have been in the shape of a female convict ship—quarrelling, fighting, thieving, destroying in private each other's property from a mere spirit of devilishness, conversation with each other most abandoned, without feeling or shame.[7]

Elizabeth Hayward retained her spirit and was not broken by her life's abrupt change in circumstances. Once she arrived in the colony she was taken into the Reverend Richard Johnson's household as a servant. No doubt this was meant to protect her from the company of the more hardened criminals—she was, after all, the youngest female convict at Port Jackson. Yet, within a year of her arrival, on 9 February 1789, she was sentenced to thirty lashes for insolence.

On the *Lady Penrhyn* Elizabeth and her fellow-prisoners had no regimented daily labour to perform. It was not until thirty years later that specific tasks were introduced on board ship, and so idleness, boredom, fear, frustration and sexual tension escalated. Disorder and mutinous behaviour quickly became part of the war of the sexes and liaisons were quick to form.

In March 1787, once the women began arriving on the *Lady Penryhn*, Governor Phillip wrote a letter of complaint to the under secretary of the admiralty:

The Situation in which the magistrates sent the women on board the *Lady Penrhyn*, stamps them with infamy—tho' almost naked, and so very filthy, that nothing but clothing them could have prevented them from perishing, and which could not be done in time to prevent a fever, which is still on board that ship, and where there are many venereal complaints, that must spread in spite of every precaution.[8]

This is not an isolated example of Phillip's paternalism towards his charges, and his concern and humane attention were to be displayed on numerous occasions.

Perhaps the women were keen to start their journey as a way to assuage their growing anxiety about the future. On the day of departure convicts were still arriving on board the ships, including the sibling pair of George, aged about thirteen, and Elizabeth Youngson, about fourteen, who embarked on the *Prince of Wales*. Both had been sentenced to death for burglary, but a timely touch of leniency made them last-minute additions to the First Fleet.

As tempting as it is to concentrate on the drama of convicts facing permanent exile in a strange land, it could make us neglect the significance of family life *transplanted* rather than transported to Sydney Cove. Examples of this are predominantly found in the families of marines, who with their wives and children sailed on the First Fleet.

History has largely ignored the four companies of marines who served at Port Jackson until the end of 1791. Any attention they have received usually focuses on the officers—on Major Ross, who would be lieutenant-governor of the colony, and his difficult relationship with his commander Arthur Phillip. Yet below officer level lies the major example of family life in the earliest years of settlement. The marines were able to maintain a continuity of family relationships because of navy regulations. These regulations permitted the wives and children of some ranks to accompany them:

> as it is usual when any regiments are sent upon service
> to his Majesty's colonies or plantations to allow them
> to take with them a certain number of women, we
> beg leave to propose that the wives of the marines

going to Botany Bay…may be allowed to embark with
them.'[9]

The number of wives permitted to accompany marines was
limited to ten per company, and about twenty-three sailed. Of
these wives, half brought children with them, fifteen in all, and
nine of the wives were pregnant on embarkation. There were
no restrictions on the number of marine children who could
accompany their parents.

The government's efforts in maintaining and transplanting
family life which the marines enjoyed is in stark contrast to that of
the convicts. But this is only correct to a degree: those ranked as
sergeant, corporal and private were permitted to bring family—
officers did not have this privilege. Major Ross saw a way to
circumvent this ruling by bringing his young son with him as a
volunteer doing duty without pay.

This dislocation of family life at officer level is easy to overlook
in favour of heart-rending accounts of convict mothers and fathers
separated from children, from partners and from community.
What is apparent is that the convicts and their guards on the First
Fleet had at least one thing in common: the distress and suffering
of separation.

If the children of convicts of the First Fleet were an overlooked
addition to the cargo they were not alone in their juvenile distress.
The sixteen children of marines were similarly omitted from the
victualling estimates. For over a month, from mid-March to mid-
April 1787, official letters passed back and forth before the simple
task of allocating provisions to this group was completed. The
strongest letter of complaint came from Major Ross who reported
a 'scene of distress' when he visited the assembling transports on
12 April 1787: 'In one of them I found a marine, his wife, and two
children living upon a ration and a half of provisions.'[10]

British marines took an active part in some of the great

eighteenth-century voyages of discovery into the Pacific and they had some experience with the convict situation before the First Fleet. In 1784 it was the marines who were posted to oversee the convicts on board the hulk *Dunkirk*. Unfortunately, their record during this posting was marred by a gross disregard of authority and the brutalisation of the convict women. The situation was so scandalous that by late 1784 the marines were entirely replaced by soldiers.

Two years later, when plans for Botany Bay were coming together, this earlier breach was apparently forgotten. It was a singular honour for the Marine Corps rather than the army to provide volunteers for this posting. Ross proudly wrote: 'This is the first instance in which the corps of marines has been employ'd in any way out of the usual line of duty...drawing the corps forth from that subordinate obscurity in which it has hitherto moved.'[11] This distinction was seen by Ross, the newly appointed commandant of the New South Wales Marine Corps, as a chance for his men to achieve parity with the army. If this was a singular honour, however, its value must have been more to the benefit of the officers than to the rank and file. Witness Captain Phillip's complaint that the marines were being sent 'in a worse state than ever troops were sent out of the kingdom even to the nearest garrison'.[12]

But because the posting was entirely outside the usual line of duty it offered unique prospects to both officers and privates. Various inducements were offered to attract volunteers, and when there were more volunteers than needed a ballot was held. In the normal course of events men were enlisted for life—the New South Wales marines were given the option of a discharge after three years' service in the colony and, later, the chance to settle on the land rather than return to England.

Among this group a number of families left for Botany Bay: there were the Chapmans, accompanied by their two daughters;

the Harmsworths, accompanied by a son and a daughter and another son born on the voyage; the Russells, with a daughter and a son born on the voyage and the Stewarts and the Youngs, both of whom had two sons.

The First Fleet undertook a voyage for which no obvious comparison exists—1500 people on an epic journey lasting over eight months. We may be reminded of the voyage of the *Mayflower* from Plymouth to establish the first permanent white colony in North America in 1620. The Pilgrim Fathers sailed in only one ship with about a hundred passengers, all who took the trip by choice, not by coercion. Their crossing took only sixty-five days, while the First Fleet took four times as long to complete its voyage.

During the first hard winter in Plymouth, Massachusetts, half of the colonists died. Rather than be faced with an equally decimating first year in Australia, Captain Phillip sent almost one third of his settlement to nearby Norfolk Island. There they were less of a burden on the colony's perilously low food supplies and failing crops. In both countries, too, the relationship the new arrivals established with the 'Indians' (a term universally used to describe the natives) would be crucial.

The final command to drop anchor in Botany Bay was a welcome sound to all ears. For the convicts confined in the cramped and fetid holds of the transports, their anticipation of landfall, of walking on solid ground again, of taking some of their children onto land for the very first time in their lives, must have been acute.

Some of the convicts presumably saw *Terra Australis* on 15 January 1788 as they neared Cape Dromedary, some 250 kilometres south of Port Jackson. Now, however, they were in the sheltered waters of Botany Bay. With hindsight we can ask: Was this liberty or restraint? Was this invasion or settlement? Was this a prison they came to or a colony? Their first sight of the land on which they were to live must have elicited a strong mixture of emotions—welcome and threatening, exciting and strange beyond all imagining. This was nothing like Rio or Cape Town. There was no evidence of civilisation. Everything was different, even sounds of the insects and the cries of the birds. And then there was the heat—for the expedition had arrived at the height of an Australian summer.

Captain Cook had rewritten the very map of their voyage only eighteen years earlier. He had transformed the Pacific itself 'from a maze of medieval misconceptions to an outline that was recognisably modern'.[13] Even so, at the level of popular imaginings, of dreams, fears and folklore, this Pacific maze still exerted as much fear as wonder. Botany Bay proved to be entirely unsuitable for settlement. There was none of the lush grassland they expected, no sheltered anchorage and a limited supply of fresh water. Phillip left Botany Bay with a scouting party and found Port Jackson a much more favourable place to start the colony. Five days later the entire Fleet set out for its new home.

When the First Fleet sailed through Sydney Heads it was the beginning of a rebirth for many of the convicts. It began the long process of turning criminals into colonists and, eventually, exiles into Australians. Thirty years later this inverted vision was used by the colony's first published poet, Barron Field. He described the land, not as part of God's initial creation, but as 'an after-birth,/Not conceiv'd in the Beginning/...But emerg'd at the first sinning'.[14]

At the time of disembarking, fornication and famine were the two constants on the First Fleeter's mind. Fornication was quickly addressed, for the convicts at least, as soon as the women were landed in the first week of February 1788. The tumultuous storm which greeted the women's arrival on land was matched by the unleashing of orgiastic passions by the male convicts. Some enterprising officers had already taken a mistress before landfall and others, including Lieutenant Ralph Clark, succumbed within the first year of settlement.

A landed community was established.

THE INFANT COLONY
CHRISTENED

In all the Crusoe-like adventures I ever read or
heard of, I do not recollect anything like it.

A convict's letter, 1790

BY benefit of a remarkable account, we can step ashore with the first
white child to disembark from the Fleet. This was the seven-year-old
son of one of the marines, most likely Edward Munday, who
ventured ashore at Botany Bay on 23 January 1788. This child was
from the *Charlotte* and was 'chaperoned' by Captain Tench, who
wrote:

> I had at this time a little boy, of not more than seven
> years of age, in my hand. The child seemed to attract
> their attention [the Aborigines] very much, for they
> frequently pointed to him and spoke to each other;
> and as he was not frightened, I advanced with him
> towards them, at the same time baring his bosom and
> shewing the whiteness of the skin. On the cloaths
> being removed they gave a loud exclamation, and one
> of the party, an old man, with a long beard, hideously

ugly, came close to us. I bade my little charge not to be
afraid, and introduced him to the acquaintance of this
uncouth personage. The Indian, with great gentleness,
laid his hand on the child's hat, and afterwards felt his
cloaths, muttering to himself all the while. I found it
necessary, however, by this time to send away the child,
as such a close connection rather alarmed him.[1]

Curiosity. Courtesy. Trepidation.

Face-to-face interactions in English society in the eighteenth
century were based on an understanding of one's status within an
extremely subtle and complex hierarchy. But in 1788 how did two
diametrically different worlds communicate? The principal means
used were gesture and touch: the natives pointed and the child
revealed his white skin; the natives exclaimed and the child was
'introduced' to them. Both sides were constrained by their own
version of good manners. A native displayed 'great gentleness' in
touching the child and all the while Captain Tench was at pains
to spare the boy too alarming and close a connection. The
manners of the eighteenth-century drawing-room were transported to a new context and purpose.

There are other subtexts here, evident in Tench's choice of
words describing the native as 'hideously ugly' and 'uncouth'. The
idea of the noble savage had been popularised by travellers' tales
from North America and the South Pacific, which depicted the
natives as living in harmony with nature and as creatures of intu-
itive wisdom. This vision was an alluring part of a sailor's landfall
and a fulsome quote from 1788 helps illuminate Tench's expectations and reactions:

Our commerce, our wealth, our customs, our arts, nay
even our knowledge, all conspire to disseminate profu-
sion, luxury, corruption, and depravity, and to destroy
that equality of condition, that unconscious dignity of

virtue, that amiable plainness of manners, which flourished in the early ages of the world, and which never fail to charm, in description, those who, in this age of splendid folly and polished villainy, retain sufficient firmness of mind to resist the fascination of custom, and to prefer the beautiful simplicity of nature to the deceitful allurements of art. Let us suppose this state of natural simplicity and equality still to exist in some favoured Island in the hospitable bosom of the Pacific Ocean.[2]

Not one of these white expectations was satisfied during this meeting in January 1788. The invaders were already exchanging romantic notions and fantasies for a sterner reality in regard to the native inhabitants and the land.

Is it at all possible to imagine that moment of cross-cultural confusion from an Aboriginal perspective? Such an attempt should not overlook the telling absence of any women, though it is understandable that no white woman ventured onto land until Phillip fixed on Sydney Cove as the site for settlement. The whole event was a meeting of men, and while this gender imbalance was obvious to the new arrivals, it was not so clear to the Aborigines.

Tribal custom presented the men of the tribe as the appropriate people to confront the intruders. But what did they think they were confronting? The clothes and shaved faces of the marines obscured their gender to Aboriginal eyes.

Three days before this meeting on the shores of Botany Bay, when the very first contact was made, the Aborigines resorted to the most basic sign language to explain their confusion. After the naked Aboriginal men had pointed to their own penises, Lieutenant King realised the problem: 'As they took us for women, not having our beards grown, I ordered one of the people to undeceive them in this particular.'[3] At the next meeting three days later,

John Hunter dubbed Aborigines the 'children of nature'. This Romantic vision was captured by Governor King's sketch titled 'A Family of New South Wales'.

the white child was equally remarkable to the Aborigines, for his skin colour as for his gender. What remains so significant about this meeting was that it was a child who acted as the intermediary between two cultures, a child who was exposed to them to reveal a new world order.

In this extraordinary face-to-face, the world of late eighteenth-century English childhood met the timeless world of Aboriginal tribal life. In the eyes of white commentators it was a meeting between two forms of childhood—their own civilised society meeting that of these 'children of nature'.[4] Further contact between white children and Aboriginal adults and children was to follow.

When they left the ship at Sydney Cove in 1788 many of these children were abandoning the only world they had known—a floating world—and encountering not just a new land but land itself. What did life hold for these children? What was their vision of their new home, its native inhabitants, its strange birds and animals, its beauties and dangers?

Four years later, after returning to England, Captain Arthur Phillip was referred to in Whitehall as 'the father of N. S. Wales'.[5] Perhaps it is more useful to view Phillip as having been, more accurately, the midwife to the infant colony. In so doing we can see a man reluctant to cut the umbilical cord to mother England thereby severing the lifeline of sustenance and parental authority.

To carry the analogy still further, it was reported that the infant colony at Sydney Cove was 'christened' on 26 January 1788—toasts were drunk and a salute fired.[6] No woman or child attended this christening ceremony as none went ashore on that landmark day. So began the appropriation of woman's procreative role by men in their assertion that they gave birth to the Australian nation.

Some provision for the women and children, however makeshift, had first to be established: land was cleared, a site marked out, sawpits dug, stockyards built and tents erected. Thereafter, the marines' wives first disembarked on 28 January from the *Prince of Wales*. Convict women and their children went ashore on the evening of 6 February. By this time, one imagines, any landfall would have been welcomed.

Some of the convict women stepped ashore in clothes kept especially for the occasion. Bowes Smyth remarked that they were 'dress'd in general very clean, & some few amongst them might be said to be well dress'd'.[7] Some primitive shelters were in place for their reception and on landing they were assigned places in the rows of tents. This simple act of disembarkation from the First Fleet marked a turning point in social and sexual relations: from segregation to cohabitation, from shipboard cliques to nascent landed community, from multiple prisons at sea to the single open prison of Sydney Cove.

These changes in status would carry with them profound psychological changes. The long journey and separation from home, family and country must have been particularly dislocating for the prisoners. Some shipboard journals were to reveal how the contact with convict women was a severe shock to some of the naive officers. Lieutenant Ralph Clark wrote:

> what a scene of whoredom is going on there in the women's camp—no sooner has one man gone in with a woman but another goes in with her—I hope the Almighty will keep me free from them as he has hither to done, but I need not be afraid as I promised you my tender Betsey I will keep my word with you—I will never have anything [to do with] any woman whatever except yourself my dear wife.[8]

Night came on. Immense storm clouds gathered.

Severe lightning threatened life itself on the night of 6 February 1788. A number of stock animals (in many eyes more precious than human life) were struck and killed as the elements conspired to rid the land of this invasion. The overheated atmosphere and louring sky promised a climax that was replicated below as human passions inflamed and the final landfall brought a release of pent-up fears and desires. Governor Phillip was well aware of what that night would bring. He gave orders that five of the women whose good conduct distinguished them from others during the voyage were to be separately landed and placed in a tent near his own. Who were these handmaidens of virtue thus segregated and, presumably, saved from the excesses of the night's abandonment? They were five of the six worthy women sent to Norfolk Island on 15 February 1788.

Any experienced sailor, all of the women, and anyone not blinded by too narrow a moral code knew what could be expected on that first night ashore. Any vision of clean, well-dressed women convicts bringing maternal values and some semblance of feminine charms ashore is not the stuff of which historical novels or popular myth-making are made. And so historians since then have seized avidly on a famous report by Bowes Smyth which recounts what can only be described as white Australia's founding 'orgy': 'The men Convicts got to them [the women convicts] very soon after they landed, & it is beyond my abilities to give a just description of the Scene of Debauchery & Riot that ensued during the night.'9

Elemental. Excessive. Riotous. It was quite a contrast to the image of restraint and civility which the first white child's tentative landing conjured up two weeks earlier.

The children's arrival in the colony can be recreated through two very different perspectives: the experience of a single child from the world of officialdom and that of the convict children. The marine's child elicited 'gentleness' and consideration from adults, white and black alike, when he disembarked. The convict children, though, were lost in a welter of activity—they were undifferentiated cargo unloaded into a world where formal manners and civility were subverted.

This tableau of Australia's founding mothers, some with infants at their breasts and young children by their sides who witnessed 'the Scene of Debauchery & Riot', was to be highlighted and repeated over the next two centuries to titillate appetites and confirm prejudices. Interestingly, the most explicit interpretation of the night's events to date was by Judith Cook in 1994: 'Young virgin girls in their mid-teens, old women long past child-bearing age, all were fair game. Men queued up to gang-rape victims held down for them by their roaring, laughing friends.'[10]

Yet for all the stage-centre position which the first report of the 'orgy' suggests, it is surprising to learn that Bowes Smyth was not even ashore that evening.[11] The surgeon remained on board the *Lady Penrhyn* in the harbour together with some of the sailors. Here he was better qualified to describe the drunken male revelry that followed the issuing of rum as sailors looked longingly towards the cove where the women bedded down for their first night on land. One such sailor, John Fisher, succumbed to his longing and swam ashore to join one of the convict women who had earlier borne his child—he paid for his night's pleasure by catching a chill and dying.

As with many of the documents that purport to give an eye-witness view of the colony, one must be aware of subjective vision, edited accounts and imaginative excess. Bowes Smyth, who wrote of 'Debauchery & Riot', was only one of a number of witnesses on the Fleet who were strongly censorious about the behaviour and morals of the convict women. But, given the opportunity to confirm their worst expectations, why are there so few accounts of the night's orgy? Captain Tench provides the only other mention of the event, in a paragraph remarkable for its rejection of moral standards under such straitened circumstances: 'While they [the convicts] were on board ship, the two sexes had been kept most rigorously apart; but, when landed, their separation became impracticable, and would have been, perhaps, wrong. Licentiousness was the unavoidable consequence.'[12]

Discipline at sea and on land were two different things and Tench's account says more than any purse-lipped moralist. It only hints at how intrusive the government eye was to be in the daily affairs of the convicts and gives us a foretaste of continuing government intervention as the convicts attempted to re-establish personal relationships, marital units and family circles.

Two hundred years later this evening achieves its most entertaining version in *The Fatal Shore*, where Robert Hughes confirms and strengthens the popular view of gender relations in the first settlement—of women as victims of male lust:

> as dusk fell, the weather burst. Tents blew away; within minutes the whole encampment was a rain-lashed bog. The women floundered to and fro, draggled as muddy chickens under a pump, pursued by male convicts intent on raping them...And as the couples rutted between the rocks...their clothes slimy with red clay, the sexual history of colonial Australia may fairly be said to have begun.[13]

Hughes' bestseller ensured that international readers were now part of the voyeuristic audience at the debauch. Surely there was more to the event than mass rape? True, the male convicts did outnumber the women by three to one, but the women should not simply be dismissed as victims, as Hughes intimates. As reported, some women made every attempt to look their best and may have been willing accomplices in an event that regrouped them among their own class after months of celibacy, and which gave them a temporary respite from official scrutiny, enabling them to reaffirm their own needs and desires.

If all one sees in that night's events is woman as victim, then we do these First Fleeters a grave injustice. If we wish to see them as contributing anything other than vice after their arrival we need to see them in relation to their children as they establish new patterns of family life, child care and mothering.

Alan Frost, an authoritative historian of the First Fleet, comments with abrupt justification that 'surprising as this scene may now seem, return voyages to England usually ended in this way'.[14] And perhaps this comment, as dismissive as it is, allows us a way into the events of that night. If there were precedents for the orgy then it becomes less a unique characteristic of convict relations and more part of sanctioned sexual practice among the lower orders generally.

In fact it wasn't just at the voyage's end that sexual restraint was relaxed. In the middle of the eighteenth century one British admiral wrote frankly of scenes encountered in ports of call:

> crowds of boats flock off with cargoes of prostitutes...
> The whole of the shocking, disgraceful transactions
> of the lower deck it is impossible to describe—the
> dirt, filth and stench; the disgusting conversation; the
> indecent, beastly conduct and horrible scenes;
> the blasphemy and swearing; the riots, quarrels, and
> fightings which often take place; where hundreds of
> men and women are huddled together in one room as
> it were, and where, in bed (each man being allowed
> only sixteen inches breadth for his hammock), they
> are squeezed between the next hammocks and must
> be witnesses of each other's actions.[15]

At the end of a voyage women could be more permanently accommodated on board; instead of being visitors they could cohabit. Their presence on the ship was tolerated under the fiction that they were legal wives and that they were simply continuing the family life so rudely interrupted by being at sea.

On the morning of 7 February 1788, Governor Phillip moved quickly to re-establish discipline and authority. He did so with ceremony, a show of arms and some plain-speaking. Not all was threatening or intimidating: part of his strategy was to offer the possibility of a brighter future. At 10 a.m. everyone was assembled on the west side of the cove, in the area designated as the marines' parade ground. The convicts sat encircled by the marines while formal commissions were read out. Few of the convicts could have been expected to understand the legal phrases or the extraordinary authority proclaimed in Arthur Phillip's name. Ralph Clark was to comment, 'I never herd of any one Single Person having So great a Power in Vested in him as the Governour has by his commission.'[16] The pomp and circumstance that followed, however, was deliberately tuned to convict understanding. In a short speech Phillip made it clear that the preceding night did not set a precedent and warned the convicts that sentries now had orders to fire at any man seen in the women's camps at night. What would be encouraged were efforts at improvement and industry and the establishment of formal relationships through marriage.

Did Governor Phillip realise that the dislocation of the convicts' lives, through their vast journey and the severing of family ties, would produce extreme psychological difficulties? The relief at a final, safe landfall followed by elemental excess quickly turned into a kind of stupor so that, according to Judge-Avocate David Collins, the convicts ceased to be 'thinking beings'.[17] It was vital that Phillip re-establish some aspects of the life they had known, and he did this by stressing marriage and the bonds of family. This formal introduction of the newcomers to their new world order created and circumscribed understanding for them at the edge of an alien continent.

Within three days of Phillip's speech a series of convict marriages started. Before the end of the month thirty couples were joined. Some married bigamously, presumably with little if any hope of ever returning to their first partners. This was divorce by distance. Divorce from their families, from their mother country, from Home.

What was happening here? Was the adoption of government-endorsed liaisons a currying of official favour? Was it a practical acceptance that home was a concept to be reworked in a new land? Whatever the case and however successful these liaisons were, they attest to the immediate establishment of marital units and family groups from the earliest days of settlement.

At its inception the infant colony numbered nearly 1500. Of these a total of forty-eight children, whose ages ranged from a few days to fourteen years, made up a juvenile population of 3.3 per cent of the total. There were seventeen mothers with twenty-three children belonging to the marine encampment and nineteen mothers with nineteen children in the convict camp. Alexander John Ross, the son of Major Ross, James Campbell, the nephew of Captain Campbell, and the colony's first orphan, Edward Parkinson, were three of six children without mothers. So, however much we may wonder at the imbalance of numbers between male and female in the settlement, the ratio of children to adults was even more skewed.

The first English census in 1801 showed that, out of a population of nine million, there were over four million children. If England was a country of young people its infant colony in 1788 most certainly was not, though within a decade it would appear to become just that. By the end of the century the proportion of children in the settlement had risen to almost 20 per cent. This growth created the mistaken impression that the colony was remarkably fertile and 'an extraordinary place for children'.[18] A number of accounts mention the supposed fecundity of the women. As one surgeon's mate wrote: 'women who were supposed past child-bearing, and others who had not been pregnant for fifteen or sixteen years, have lately become mothers'.[19]

For all the lowly status of its passengers, the voyage of the First Fleet was most significantly a voyage of discovery. None of the convicts (and few of the seamen) could have had much idea of the geographical reality of their landfall. Colourful mariners' fables and popular accounts of monsters, alien races and mythic beasts would have exercised and excited the minds of many of the voyagers.

Ignorance. Superstition. Heresy. Wild imaginings were perhaps all the convicts had with which to form a picture of their destination. Indeed, Captain Tench 'found the convicts particularly happy in fertility of invention, and exaggerated descriptions'.[20] In this they were probably matched by the sailors and marines aboard, for up to the eve of departure from England what authoritative works on Australia had been published? The limited knowledge of one of the actual First Fleet convicts speaks for most of them: 'a great Number is a going a Broad to a Iland that was Found by Captain Coke and Uninhabited only by Indians'.[21]

A novel like Daniel Defoe's *Robinson Crusoe*, first published in 1719, would have been a touchstone for the fears and expectations of many of the First Fleeters. At the most basic level a primitive acquaintance with adventure stories, folklore and sailors' tall tales was their only preparation for the exotic and the fearful. Thus, in 1790, one of the convicts wrote back to England: 'To give a just description of the hardships that the meanest of us endure, and the anxieties suffered by the rest, is more than I can pretend to. In all the Crusoe-like adventures I ever read or heard of, I do not recollect anything like it.'[22]

All this is to say that the common imagination had sailed to such remote regions in advance of the First Fleet—in a way the popular imagination had visited Botany Bay before 1788. And later that year the surgeon Dr Worgan described his rambles around Sydney Harbour in the company of his 'Man Friday'.[23] It is easy then to imagine that on their journey to Botany Bay many of the voyagers must have speculated, frightened and amazed themselves and the children with stories drawn from folklore and popular reading.

A year later and back in England, the public displayed great interest in accounts of the young settlement. A long procession of articles, pamphlets and journals were published, including that of Lieutenant Watkin Tench. Some first-hand accounts of antipodean wonders seemed no less strange than utter fabrications designed to fascinate those at Home. Perhaps as early as 1790 an English broadside described and illustrated 'a wonderful large wild man or monstrous giant brought from Botany Bay'. Similar accounts included sea serpents and the one-eyed Cyclops as suggested denizens of *Terra Incognita* and its surrounding seas. Frightening and convincing fantasies like these haunted the dreams of those on the First Fleet as much as the British public.

The First Fleeters' communal fantasies were never recorded apart from a later belief that on escaping they could walk overland to China. Any interest or acknowledgment of such wild and ignorant imaginings would have been unthinkable to their pragmatic Georgian overseers, but they afford us a chance to recover something of the convicts' mental landscape. There was, in fact, one world of journeying for Captain Phillip and his educated officers with their meticulous entries in logs and journals, and quite another for the convicts.

'A DESCRIPTION of a wonderful large WILD MAN, or monstrous GIANT, BROUGHT
FROM BOTANY BAY' is the title appended to this woodcut from an English broadside,
c. 1790. Graphic fantasies like this one preoccupied the British populace as well as
First Fleeters.

There is no journal, diary or cache of letters by any convict on the First Fleet. They had survived the journey across the world, and in begining to create a new life in a new land had to confront unimaginable fears and anxieties.

NORFOLK ISLAND

Poor Devils how they are Kick about from one
place to another.

Lieutenant Ralph Clark, 1790

WITHIN three weeks of proclaiming a settlement at Port Jackson,
Governor Phillip sent a handpicked group of twenty-three
men, women and children to what had been described as a 'place
fit for angels and eagles'.[1] This was Norfolk Island, first
'discovered' by Captain Cook in 1774. French explorers later
explained their inability to breach the island's formidable coast-
line by resorting to such dramatic exaggeration—in truth there
was nothing angelic about the First Fleeters who arrived there in
March 1788.

Norfolk Island had first attracted the admiralty's interest as a
place where flax and pine trees grew in abundance. Both were
vital to Britain's naval strength: the flax to be woven into sails and
the timber for masts and ship-building. The island also had
another significant advantage—no native population to usurp or
to compete with for resources. Lord Sydney had instructed Phillip
quite clearly before he sailed: 'You are, as soon as circumstances

admit of it, to send a small establishment thither and to secure the same to us to prevent it being occupied by the subjects of any other European power.'[2]

This early enthusiasm for Norfolk Island as a source of naval supplies proved to be ill-founded: the pine trees were unsuitable and the flax proved different from the European variety of the plant. Furthermore, the extreme danger in reaching a safe anchorage at the island was to bedevil many of the colony's efforts.

When Philip Gidley King, the island's first administrator, arrived with his founding 'family' in 1788, it took five days of searching before a landing could be effected. King was an ambitious administrator and his reports back to Port Jackson were designed to justify the trust inherent in his appointment and the value of the new settlement. These exaggerated reports encouraged Governor Phillip to send a large number of convicts to the island at the beginning of 1790.

If King failed to emphasise just how treacherous any landing could be at the island, he also neglected to depict the limited resources of its food supply. The result, in early 1790, was that two infant colonies existed, Port Jackson and Norfolk Island, each with around 700 men, women and children. Both settlements were to face real starvation for a time.

Before the end of 1788 another boatload arrived at Norfolk Island from Port Jackson. It included two children belonging to convict mothers. These children have never been firmly identified and were almost certainly not First Fleeters. The island's first births occurred very soon after: appropriately enough Philip Gidley King's son Norfolk King was the first child born there on 8 January 1789.

This was followed by the first of Olivia Gascoigne's thirteen children on 2 March 1789. It was also on this day that the first known children from the First Fleet arrived to settle Norfolk

Island: the orphan Edward Parkinson and Mary Fowles. These two were designated as 'public wards' by Captain Phillip and were allocated the produce from five acres to sustain them. The transfer of this pair to the island seems to have been considered an act of philanthropic exile from the unsuitable environment of Port Jackson.

Edward Parkinson may have been as young as four at this time. Mary Fowles had accompanied her convict mother on the First Fleet and was around six by the time she arrived at the island. She was sent there as a means of separating her from her mother, who Judge-Advocate Collins described as 'a woman of abandoned character'.[3] Another young arrival with this group was the convict George Youngson, about fifteen years old. Youngson was a last addition to the First Fleet: in what must have been a confusing and frighteningly sudden series of events he found himself sentenced to death in March, reprieved to transportation in April and embarked in May 1787. After these arrivals, it was another year before more children from the First Fleet swelled the island's numbers.

Governor Phillip appears to have viewed the island as something of a sanctuary, which inspired him to divide his populace into roughly equal halves. He listed the benefits of what was, in the settlement's terms, a large-scale migration:

> The advantages I expected by sending away such a number of people was from the little garden ground they would leave and which would assist those who remained, and the fish which might be caught in the winter would go the further. At the same time those sent to Norfolk Island would have resources in the great abundance of vegetables raised there and in fish and birds, which this settlement [Port Jackson] could not afford them...[4]

Unfortunately, Phillip's optimism, based on Lieutenant King's reports from the island, was misplaced, and life there was to be as desperate and as near starvation as it was back in Port Jackson. If, in fact, this significant number of people had not been removed from the first settlement, starvation would have been a real risk for the entire colony.

Sydney Harbour, 6 March 1790. The *Sirius* and the *Supply* set sail for Norfolk Island with about 350 people aboard including seven children from the First Fleet—Ann Smith, Henrietta Langley and Alexander Ross came on the *Sirius* and Jane Jones, Esther Abrahams and John Hart on the *Supply*. Also on the *Sirius*, and now presumably aged fifteen, was John Hudson.[5] It was a fine morning, 'moderate weather little wind' and an auspicious start to yet another chapter in the lives of these young voyagers.[6]

Before the ships managed to clear the harbour though, the *Sirius* was almost wrecked on North Head. In Lieutenant Clark's words, it was only by 'great good fortune' that danger was averted: 'the Ship would have been in pi[e]ces in a few minutes from the great Sea that was breaking on the Rocks and the most of us on board would have been lost.'[7] It was a terrifying reacquaintance with life on board ship. After clearing the Heads, most of the passengers succumbed to seasickness for two or three days: 'Between decks there is Such a disagreeable Smell from the women that are Sea Sick that it is a nuff to Suffocate one.'[8]

On the morning of 13 March, the island's forbidding cliffs and pounding surf made landing difficult. Landing adjacent to the settlement was impossible and the ships proceeded around the island. Once again there was a sudden brush with disaster. The *Sirius* landed all the marines and then followed with a boatload of women and children: 'But while the[y] were landing them a

Sea Brok[e] into the Boat which frightend them very much,' Clark reported. 'I wonder that the Boat [was] not lost and every body in her for the women would not Sit Still but made a terible noise both them and the children but the[y] all got Save on Shore.'9 After this ordeal there were no comforts in sight—the settlement was close to eight kilometres away along a very rough road and the women and children had no choice but to sleep overnight in the open.

The new commandant of the island, Major Robert Ross, who was to replace Lieutenant King while he was in England reporting on the difficulties the settlements faced, landed the next day before rough weather forced both ships out to sea. When the gale moderated on 19 March another attempt to land was made close to the settlement. On shore, a fully raised flag indicated that landing conditions were favourable. The *Supply* off-loaded its provisions safely but, as soon as the longboats from the *Sirius* were loaded, the wind then shifted. Everything was thrown into confusion. The *Supply* managed to tack and headed out to sea. The *Sirius*, a larger ship with a captain who had never been to the island before, ran onto a reef: 'In Less than 10 Minutes the Masts were all over the side, the Ship an intire Wreck.'10

While we can never know John Hudson's role during this disaster it is clear he was a witness to the event. He may even have assisted in the salvaging process, and hauled on the line that stretched from the wreck to one of the island's imposing pine trees.

It was fortunate that the wreck occurred close to land—no lives were lost and many of the supplies, though not personal possessions, were saved. As the turbulent sea calmed, two convicts volunteered to swim out to the wreck and liberate the livestock. They then proceeded to claim what they considered a well-earned reward: they also liberated the ship's cellar. Soon they were so drunk that they set fire to the very wreck beneath their feet.

At first the new commandant made a point of praising the salvage attempt. A few days later, however, he found it necessary to issue a proclamation against those who 'in a most scandalous and infamous manner...robbed and plundered' items from the wreck.[11] Robert Ross had found the perfect situation in which to assert his full authority and promptly declared martial law.

By the middle of May 1790 short rations were introduced. Children over twelve months were to receive half the adult ration: 1½ pounds of flour (680 grams), ¾ pound of salt beef or pork (340 grams) and ½ pound of rice (225 grams). Further reductions followed in July and August. After two years of tension while he played a subordinate role to Governor Phillip, Ross was in a position that suited his autocratic nature. He took personal satisfaction in issuing verbose and stern proclamations and implemented his own ideas on how a settlement should be run. He decided that the 'Articles of War for the better government of all his Majesty's forces' should be proclaimed in public.[12] Life for John Hudson and his companions was to become distinctly more regimented.

At the beginning of 1790 most of the children from the First Fleet were under six, though they were still quite capable, and indeed necessary, helpers in foraging for food. They supplemented their meagre rations with edible wild plants and pine nuts, may have helped their mothers drying out the flour and rice salvaged from the *Sirius*, gathered firewood and thatch and prepared the cleared acreage for planting. Towards the end of that first difficult year it is also likely they helped pick caterpillars off the crops.

In late April there was the fortuitous arrival of thousands of petrels. They appeared each night for four months, and saved the settlement from near starvation. In one night alone almost 6000 birds were killed: 'a little before sunset the air was thick with them as gnats are on a fine summer's evening in

England'.[13] No sooner did this unexpected visitation come to an end than it was followed by another unwelcome one—a severe plague of caterpillars and grubs that drastically damaged the crops.

By the end of 1790, as advances were followed by losses, Ross devised a plan for the convicts to maintain themselves rather than rely on supplies from the public stores. He divided them into groups, allocated them land and gave them time off to cultivate their own acreage, thus encouraging the formation of small family units and the development of some sense of personal future and community:

> The convicts who are indulged with the privilege of maintaining themselves shall be classed together, and not less than three in a family, women and children included. And for the further encouragement of such male convicts as are desirous to maintain the females, such females shall not be called upon by the public to do any work, except in hoeing the corn upon an appearance of rain, or picking the caterpillars or grubs from the corn, or any other work of evident necessity.[14]

Was this the formation of self-sufficient and industrious model families? What remains unclear is whether the women were free to choose with whom they lived or if they were allocated partners by Ross. In any event, the plan sadly overestimated both the convicts' capacity and willingness to work. Grinding hunger made few, if any, of the people eager to add yet more work to the amount required as servants of the Crown. A significant number preferred to pillage, reverting to a savagery which matched the island's terrain and situation: 'They left the public works and took to the woods in order to make a descent by night upon the houses and gardens of private individuals as well as the public grounds, where many of them have supported themselves for several months independent of the store.'[15]

And so Ross's vision of family groups and subsistence farming was subject to abuse. On returning to his post as lieutenant-governor of the island in 1792, Philip Gidley King wrote to Governor Phillip about the convict farmers:

> I knew it to be the intention of many of them to gain what they could from their grounds, and when they had realised enough to carry them off the island, to leave their families, which would be a great burthen to the public. Some of them hoped that if they cleared their ground they might be permitted to make their grants over to their wives or their friends, by which the industrious individual would suffer greatly, as fifty of the best and most desirable lots would, in time, become the property of abandoned women, burthened with children.[16]

Throughout Major Ross's last year of office on Norfolk Island, a number of incidents involving children could be seen as part of a general breakdown of discipline and authority. The first of these incidents involved Ross's young son.

Of the nine children from the First Fleet, the one whose status was most altered by the move to Norfolk Island was Alexander John Ross, aged about nine. As the son of the new commandant he was in a more privileged position than the one he occupied at Port Jackson. Even so, there were no boys of comparable age for Alexander John Ross to associate with; no-one like his friend James Campbell, who had sailed with him on the First Fleet. (Campbell was equally bereft of young companionship back in Port Jackson with his uncle.) Major Ross and Captain Campbell had been bound together by the enmity they felt towards Governor Phillip and their constant dissatisfaction with the settlement. While Ross was the natural choice as commandant for the island, his removal from Port Jackson served another purpose: it was a convenient way of breaking the alliance between Ross and Campbell. Unfortunately, it also separated their two young boys from each other's company.

On Norfolk Island the young Ross was now a second lieutenant. In this lonely place he had to consider his father's new and pre-eminent position and take his own rank seriously. This position was not that of an indulged child whose father allowed him to wear a uniform. Indeed, the only indulgence that we know of came not from the boy's father but from Lieutenant Clark, who constantly and affectionately referred to the child in his journal as 'little John'. No doubt Clark was reminded of his own son Ralph whom he had not seen for over two years. Alexander John was a frequent companion on Clark's day trips to the outlying settlement of Charlotteville. One imagines that the boy found this companionship welcome after that of his 'self-important and almost totally humourless' father.[17]

Major Ross was 'such a strong character that he [would]…allow no one under him to be comfortable', and whether in Port Jackson or on Norfolk Island he was often responsible for provoking conflict and creating factions in the close-knit community.[18] Young Alexander John was ultimately, and perhaps inevitably, caught in the crossfire on at least one occasion. One example of this resulted from the continuing conflict between his father and Captain Hunter. Their antagonism to each other had been exhibited before either arrived at Norfolk Island. The wreck of the *Sirius* stranded Hunter at the island for ten months. With the former commandant and his replacement thrust together every day, the potential for discord was extreme.

In February 1791 Alexander John Ross was said to have been the cause of the last upset when he announced that his father was reporting Hunter to the admiralty. Although the boy later denied the story, the constant bickering, jealousy and discord between the two men must have created a complex web of ever-changing loyalties, of recriminations and counter-recriminations, which could hardly be understood by a child.

Hunter was not the only one unimpressed with Ross. In the ranks of both convicts and marines there were grievances. Punishments for all levels of the community fill the Norfolk Island pages of Lieutenant Clark's journal, and as many as 500 lashes were ordered for one convict alone. This is where we find the last reliable mention of John Hudson. In February 1791 he was 'Punished with 50 Lashes for being out of his hutt after nine oClock'.[19] Later that same year the convict boy Samuel Cooley, fourteen, was given '13 Lashes on the Backside' for stealing.[20] Ross's harsh regime was no more evident than when he had these two youngest male convicts lashed.

In July 1791 a former marine who had already been sentenced for raping a nine-year-old girl committed the same crime again. The commandant's decisive action after the wreck of the *Sirius* kept the island under strict and effective control, but by 1792 there was escalating unrest and a complete social breakdown on all fronts—convict, marine and military. The incidents with the children were but part of a general malaise.

The first day of Ross's final year as commandant opened with one of the pregnant convict women being confined in irons. This set the tone for the rest of Ross's stay: a gaol was built, at least eight court martials were held and the marines were described as 'ripe for rising against any Authority' and likely to shed 'a great dele of Blood'.[21] One convict went mad and had to be restrained and Ross was accused of cruelty in letters to Port Jackson. When Phillip King returned to the island to resume his former role he was to find 'discordant strife in every person's countenance'.[22]

When King returned in November 1791 he was a different man. It was not simply his promotion to commander's rank in the navy and lieutenant-governor of the island; King had also married and his wife was expecting their first child. (His two illegitimate sons by his former convict mistress had been acknowledged and would receive a good education in England.) The significant difference here was that the island now had a First Family at its head. The effect of this on the community's fortunes, particularly with regard to conditions for children, was considerable.

With the help of his compassionate wife Anna, King set up a school and an orphanage in his new term of office. Collins wrote: 'A school House was built, and a Careful Woman was appointed to take Charge of, and instruct the Children; among whom are several who have been deserted by their parents, and left a Burthen to the Island.'[23] King established a fund for the care of these orphans and all fines and forfeitures were paid to the chaplain for the children's benefit. Then in December 1793 King taxed alcohol imports 'to make such Quantitys serviceable to the Children among whom are many helpless Orphans, deserted by their Parents'.[24]

Once again we have to search diligently through the official records to catch a glimpse of John Hudson. He becomes increasingly obscured by the multifarious activities necessary in the establishment of a convict colony. We even lose our hold on firm evidence of his continued existence.

The notoriety Norfolk Island gained over the next hundred years for cruelty, suffering and depravity, cannot fail to make us wonder if John Hudson was victimised at this last stage of his recorded life. The ugly reality is that sexual abuse was a likely threat in this isolated community. It is true that there is no evidence of homosexual rape on Norfolk Island during Hudson's stay, but there are enough reports from there early in the next century for us to suspect that such an ordeal would have been another erosion of his childhood and his humanity.

In 1847 the island's superintendent referred to 'some of the wretched lads previously known as "colonial women"'.[25] The evasive language of even earlier reports cannot conceal that threat to young convicts like John Hudson: 'At night the sleeping-wards are very cess-pools of unheard-of vices.'[26] An 1840s parliamentary report was more direct in its language:

> The young have no chance of escaping from abuse, and even forcible violation is resorted to. To resist can hardly be expected, in a situation so utterly removed from, and lamentably destitute of, protection. A terrorism is sternly and resolutely maintained, to revenge, not merely exposure but even complaint.[27]

Certainly John Hudson faced such threats in Newgate Prison, on board the *Mercury* and probably during the long voyage to Australia. His unknown sufferings on Norfolk Island are but another chapter in a saga forever lost. Did John recall the parting words of the judge at his trial in the Old Bailey? Did he remember that his sentence was passed in an effort to remove him 'from destruction'?[28] In the small settlement on Norfolk Island did Hudson feel saved or abandoned?

THE DEVIL AT BOTANY BAY

NORFOLK Island was not unique in its treatment of convicts, coupled with its ugly threat of child abuse. Back in Sydney Cove there were signs that this outpost was to be a noisy and precocious child of empire, whose development would not proceed according to strict rules of upbringing.

The earliest extant charts, maps and drawings provide us with a view of the infant settlement growing lustily in the first months of 1788. Despite the forward planning and Governor Phillip's careful positioning of cliques around the cove there were unforeseen disruptions to his grand plan caused by the numbers of people involved and the sheer novelty of what was being undertaken. 'The spot which had so lately been the abode of silence and tranquillity was now changed to that of noise, clamour, and confusion.'[1]

In this alien land, parents must have felt the threat, to themselves as well as to their children, of being lost in the encircling bush, attacked by natives, devoured by unimaginable monsters or simply forgotten by the rest of the world they had left behind. There were, however, less exotic but more likely dangers for their children that lurked within the exiled community itself, dangers which have always haunted the vulnerable world of childhood and which were no different from what would have been feared back Home. Hunger, deprivation, neglect and abuse were all still possible and far more likely to surface in a community without established support structures. There were no extended family networks of uncles, aunts and grandparents for these children, nor were there the charities which, however inadequate, provided some small relief for their suffering. These deprivations placed new responsibilities on all the families and social units, free or convict, in the colony.

This settlement had to lay the foundations for a new life using an alienated group of criminals facing hunger and a fear of the unknown. Late eighteenth-century modes of decorum, deference and 'noblesse oblige', were to be expected in polite society, but for these 'damn'd whores' and convict men such refinement was out of place. And, if the examples of the treatment of two First Fleet children were anything to go by, the new settlement maintained the same age-old horrors—whether towards child or adult—of rape and abuse.

Of the earliest court cases in the colony, two concerned the rape of young girls—two of the twenty-one girls under fourteen from the First Fleet. Although their story is not atypical, its retelling reminds us today that the sanctity of childhood has always been at risk and was perhaps even more susceptible in this frontier society.

Elizabeth Chapman, an eight-year-old, was raped in 1789 by a marine. Ann Smith, eleven, claimed she was raped by a free settler in 1796. A close reading of both cases conveys more than the distress and suffering of these children—it gives us an insight into a hidden corner of colonial society. Our sense of outrage is not the same as that raised through stories of convicts lashed or starved. The rape of a child is an indelible horror, even if it happened some two hundred years ago.

On 23 August 1789 the first recorded case of child rape in the colony occurred. Henry Wright, 'not having the Fear of God before his Eyes...did ravish and carnally know' Elizabeth Chapman.[2] This child, the daughter of a marine, had accompanied her parents and sister to New South Wales on the First Fleet, possibly on the *Prince of Wales*. Henry Wright, also a marine, arrived on the same ship with his wife and infant daughter and the two families could not have failed to know one another.

At the trial, on 10 September 1789, the court was initially concerned with testing the child's sense of right and wrong:

Q. How old are you?

A. A little more than eight.

Q. Do you know that it is wrong to speak an untruth?

A. Yes.

Q. What will happen to you if you do?

A. Go to the Devil.

Q. Where do you expect to go if you speak Truth?

A. To Heaven.

Q. Can you say your Catechism?

A. Yes.

Q. The Lord's Prayer?

A. Yes.[3]

The child dutifully recited the prayer—'deliver us from Evil'—and thus satisfied the court as to her honesty, integrity and Christian upbringing. She was duly sworn in and delivered her testimony.

It was a late afternoon in the settlement, a Sunday afternoon, a time for resting or for visiting the neighbours. Elizabeth Chapman had been invited to take an afternoon cup of tea with the wife of one of the marines. It was a simple enough event, one which celebrated domestic calm and social ease. It helped re-establish a civilised interchange half a world away from its British model. Spring was soon to arrive and presumably there was still a chill in the air which a cup of tea would help to temper.

Through such simple habits the officers' cliques settled into a genteel lifestyle, re-establishing a small world of eighteenth-century ceremony. Alongside the celebration of official ceremonies in the colony were these simpler, informal and domestic social interactions.

Lest we imagine that such domestic pastimes were enacted in some eighteenth-century drawing-room, however, before the tea could be served Elizabeth and her hostess had to visit the wife of another marine to borrow the cups and saucers. On the way there, they were met by Elizabeth's little sister Jane.

So far the story reads like a popular tract of the time which stressed family values, Christian sentiment and simple domestic pleasures. Yet all was not well—this was a thin veneer of civilisation all too easily pierced. Henry Wright was to be 'moved and seduced by the Instigation of the Devil' and to overturn this image of social ceremony.[4]

Jane carried a message from Wright that he had flowers for Elizabeth. Her hostess gave Elizabeth leave to go—the requisite social courtesies observed—and she was lured away by the promise of flowers. When she arrived at Wrights' house he was there alone, but suddenly (and presumably unexpectedly) his wife returned with some visitors. Not to be thwarted, he suggested a walk to get Elizabeth out of the house:

> when he came to Cockle Bay, the Prisoner said, 'Betty shall we play?'…she said no and ran away from him…he came after her…and overtook her…then the

> Prisoner sat down upon the Ground and put her upon his lap…she saw him unbutton his Breeches…he put her astraddle across him…he took up her Petticoats…he then put his Private Parts where she makes water…he hurt her very much.[5]

The abrupt recital of events amply conveys the outrage and pain experienced by this young child. Unlike many historical retellings from the earliest days of settlement, events like these, involving children and families rather than more renowned figures, continue to move us and engage our sympathy today.

We are brought up with a sudden start when it is stated that Wright's wife 'was sitting a little Distance from them'.[6] Could she have failed to see or hear what happened? When the child later says she will tell her mother, Wright declared that 'he does not care'.[7] His subsequent action, however, belied this insouciance and was a mixture of bribery and threat: 'He told her he would give her a Doll—which he did that evening…He said if she did [tell], he would smack her Backside.'[8]

A full week passed with the child afraid to tell anyone for fear of being beaten. By her silence she was isolated from the companionship of her sex and from the sympathy of her family. When her mother testified it was to claim that 'she has never known her Daughter to tell her a Lie in her Life'.[9] And yet the child's very silence was kind of lie. The court proceedings were almost finished when Elizabeth's mother introduced a startling item into her testimony: 'She had forewarned her of going with the Prisoner— had heard he had the Character of doing such things with children.'[10] An informal network among the wives of the marines must have spread news of Wright's 'Character' throughout the settlement.

How was it then that, in the light of this opinion, more care was not taken in guarding the children from this man? The day's proceedings were abruptly terminated, as if to give the court time to assess this provocative statement. The next day the case was dealt with in less than a full page of court records. The verdict, 'Guilty—Death' appears above the florid signature of the judge-advocate. Justice was done.

The subsequent history of Henry Wright proved that he was an habitual offender. Henry Wright's death sentence was commuted to transportation to Norfolk Island for life: eighteen months later he committed the same crime on Elizabeth Gregory, a ten-year-old from the Second Fleet. This time his punishment was to run the gauntlet between the islanders as they beat and reviled him. There is no record of the extent of his injuries, or, surprisingly, of a further court sentence.

During her husband's exile on Norfolk Island Henry Wright's wife formed a new liaison with another marine and left the colony. Within four years Wright was granted a conditional pardon. He returned to Port Jackson in 1808 and fathered a new family. By the time he died at eighty, in 1837, his earlier notoriety had been replaced by a more acceptable distinction: that of the longest surviving marine from the First Fleet.

The last word on this sorry tale is from the judge-advocate, David Collins: 'This was an offence that did not seem to require an immediate example; the chastity of the female half of the settlement had never been so rigid, as to drive men to so desperate an act...'[11] It was a strange assessment of the crime and resulted in a markedly inadequate sentence. Judge Collins's words reveal a total misunderstanding of the crime. He reasoned that an 'immediate example' to the community such as hanging was unwarranted; that none of the men needed to rape a child when the morals of the adult females were so free.

What is difficult to overlook in the verdict is the dismissive attitude to the 'female part of the settlement'—they are not even referred to as 'women' and were undifferentiated according to age. Collins saw rape as a 'desperate' act, as if the child provided a last resort for sexual release, yet it seems clear the convicted marine desired a child rather than an adult.

The second known rape case involving a child from the First Fleet illuminates a seldom-seen corner of colonial life and reveals attitudes to children, to sexuality and to class. Ann Smith arrived in the colony as a two-year-old with her convict mother of the same name. Ann jnr had been born in prison and accompanied her mother to the *Dunkirk* hulk for three months before embarkation. Between March 1790 and March 1793 they lived on Norfolk Island where they may have met a free settler, Andrew Hamilton Hume, who was later the father of the famous explorer.

Hume had been a superintendent of convicts on the Thames hulks and this experience, together with a knowledge of farming and flax processing, recommended him to the authorities. He arrived in the colony in mid-1790 and took up a post on Norfolk Island in charge of a convict workforce attempting to harvest and process the flax plant. He had once fought a duel in England and was regarded as an argumentative character. Soon after his arrival on the island he clashed with Major Ross, who was to comment, 'What a Rascal this Hume is.'[12]

In 1793 Hume sailed for Port Jackson. The young Ann Smith and her mother were on the same ship and the child was later to be employed as a servant in Hume's household. Then, in 1796, Hume was charged with attempting 'feloniously to ravish' the eleven-year-old child:

> He placed her on a Chair, pulled her Petticoats up, unbuttoned his Breeches & put his Nastiness between her legs, he put her to Pain, she did not cry out, being her Master, she was afraid he would beat her...she told him she would tell her Mammy of him, he said

> she must not, she is quite certain he put his Private
> Parts and not his Finger, he had never done so
> before.[13]

The phrase 'put his Nastiness between her Legs' conveys the repugnance the child felt and the earthy vigour of her accusation.

What was particularly remarkable was Hume's behaviour immediately thereafter: 'He was going out after this & desired her to set the Tea things & stay to tea, but having set the Tea Things she went home.'[14] This was a perversion of that same ceremony of social grace and amiability that figured so predominantly in Elizabeth Chapman's story. Hume attempted to maintain control of the situation by re-establishing the master–servant relationship, and at the same time confounding it by asking his servant to stay to tea.

The child lived at the 'Bottom of the Town of Parramatta' and once home 'felt immediately an uneasiness between her Legs'.[15] After a few days her pain grew worse and she finally told her mother—'at this time she could hardly walk'.[16] At the end of her testimony the accused himself was permitted to question the child:

> Was it the first time she had had Connection with any
> Man?
>
> No.[17]

Hume's defence then began. He called soldiers from the New South Wales Corps to discredit the child, and even began to suggest that she was a known and experienced child whore. What are we to make of Ann's answer to Hume's question? The very wording may have confused the child and must have intimidated her.

Ann's mother was then called and through her account the simple domestic arrangements of early colonial society can be seen. The child shared her parents' bed that night because visitors had taken up all other space. The next morning her mother was alarmed at the sight of marks on her daughter 'which she thought ought not to have been'.[18] Ann admitted that 'some Man had had to do with her' but was afraid to name her attacker for fear of being beaten.[19] The mother tried to reassure her, saying that 'nobody should beat her for telling the truth'.[20] When this failed to elicit an explanation it was followed by threats until Ann reluctantly named the accused. The child was immediately taken to Sydney for a medical, and presumably, legal opinion. The accused actually followed them there, and endeavoured to secure their silence with a substantial bribe of £15.

The medical testimony was then offered at the trial, yet only served to confuse the matter further. The first surgeon who examined the child was uncertain of his opinion: 'I would judge better by another Examination.'[21] The court waited while three surgeons subjected the poor child to yet another test there and then, and concluded that 'she had not been entered although the discharge was venereal'.[22]

After this somewhat contradictory testimony the accused had his turn. He presented himself as almost 'A Father to the Child', and claimed that 'he had 18 Months since discovered a Connexion between her & another Man'. With fatherly concern he informed the mother 'and would have brought him to Justice, but the Mother would not suffer it'.[23] A major aspect of Hume's defence was to present a picture of domestic harmony to the court; to show that the child enjoyed and benefited from the generosity and care of her employer. For this reason one of Hume's servants added a description of simple household chores, of washing and folding clothes. The child was pictured as an onlooker to all of this, playing with puppies on the floor and treated to some sugar candy. It was furthermore claimed that she was never out of the company of these servants whenever Hume was in the house.

It is clear that Hume marshalled his witnesses with great care. His own brief testimony did not allude to the charge of rape at all, nor did he refute the offering of a bribe. Instead, he let his servants, a newly arrived convict woman, a soldier and others destroy the reputation of his accuser. There was even some evidence that suggested that Ann was being groomed as a child prostitute: 'the little girl came to her at Parramatta & she saw her go under a rug with a soldier…She saw him come from the Rug, button his trousers and say that the girl was fit for a small Man but not for a large one.'[24] The same witness testified that this was the second soldier to complain that the child was too young. Are we to believe that this convict woman was a bawd procuring children for prostitution and using her rooms as a brothel? Yet another witness claimed that 'the Child has frequently come into the place where he lives, and has pulled up her Cloathes and offered herself to him for Tobacco'.[25] The case for the defence finally concluded with more damning testimony from a soldier that 'the little Girl, has been often at the Barracks where he lives…She was a forward Girl—she has often come & stood between his Legs'.[26]

The trial ended and a verdict of not guilty was delivered, but much remains unanswered. The modern researcher is forced to re-evaluate the case in the certainty that beyond the medical investigation there was no real analysis of conflicting reports, of recriminations and counter-recriminations, of evidence obscured or deliberately slanted. No such investigative procedure was a standard part of the legal process of the day. The machinery of eighteenth-century justice worked far too quickly for anything other than a cursory assessment of the case.

Hume's witnesses managed to discredit the child's reputation absolutely while the prosecution offered no rebuttal. Yet it would not be difficult to demolish Hume's reputation as an honest citizen. What the case did not reveal was that Hume had been in court earlier that same year. As government storekeeper at Parramatta he had been suspended on a charge of defrauding the store. Although acquitted and reinstated, soon after this he was finally dismissed for unspecified 'irregularities of conduct'.[27] Later still, he was dismissed from the post of superintendent of livestock and was described by Governor King as a 'worthless character'.[28] Once again Hume was reinstated briefly, but soon dismissed under suspicion of dishonesty. While this history of fraud does not make him a rapist, it substantially reduces his credibility as an honest and stalwart citizen.

If colonial society was prepared to believe the worst of the convict women's morals, and that someone like Hume from the ruling class was to be favoured with the court's indulgence, then the verdict of this trial is no surprise. Although Ann Smith snr had served her sentence by this time, she was hardly on the same class level as Hume. Furthermore, her daughter, although legitimately born, would always be tainted with her mother's past status.

These two cases seem to indicate that child rape in the colony may have been viewed with less abhorrence than today—or perhaps this was dependent on the class of person who committed the crime. A few years later, in 1805, it is interesting to note that a convict convicted of raping a child of five or six was sentenced to 300 lashes and five years' government labour.[29]

Cases of child rape, whether proved or disproved, reinforced popular conceptions of the colony as depraved and desperate. They also showed how vulnerable the world of childhood could be and how easily the devil could find employment at Botany Bay.

FAMILY BLESSINGS

Receive me, lads! I'll go with you
Hunt the black swan and kangaroo,
And in New Holland we'll presume
Old England with some elbow room.
Across the mountains we will roam;
And each man make himself a home:
Or, if old habits ne'er forsaking,
Like clock-work of the Devil's making,
Ourselves inveterate rogues should be,
We'll have a virtuous progeny...

Samuel Taylor Coleridge, 'The Delinquent
Travellers', 1824

An extraordinary contrast, both to John Hudson's punishment on Norfolk Island and to the distressing accounts of child rape in the colony, is found in the continuing story of the Kable family. They were blessed with colonial advantage, opportunity and social advancement far beyond any expectation they could have had in Norwich Castle Gaol. The young Henry Kable's life offers the most complete documented story of any child who sailed on the First Fleet.

The Kables were the most celebrated convict family on the First Fleet and had an uncanny ability to remain in the public eye to great advantage. On landing at Port Jackson they became one of five couples joined in the first wedding ceremony held in Australia on 10 February 1788. No doubt their young son was a witness to this event.

Attitudes to marriage and cohabitation were widely divergent at the time. Fine moral distinctions were a luxury unavailable to the lower classes. To designate their child as 'illegitimate' was merely to apply a term from a foreign world of property and inheritance. The loose form of union which had been practised for centuries by many of the poor and landless people was redefined in 1753. The Clandestine Marriage Act of that year refused to recognise private ceremonies as a form of marriage unless officiated in a church. The children of such unions were deemed illegitimate and, as a result, historians find a steep rise in the rate of illegitimate births in England after the 1750s.[1]

The prosperity that the Kables enjoyed fuelled a growing belief in Britain that transportation to Botany Bay was, in some instances, less a punishment and more a means to prosperity, social elevation and opportunity. In Governor Hunter's words, 'Some of the very dregs of those who have been sent here convicts are now in possession of their horses and chaise, servants, and other symbols of wealth.'[2] The Kable family's success after just a decade in the settlement was a tribute to entrepreneurial energy and colonial opportunity as much as it was to their determined sense of survival. What other story could match that of Henry Kable snr, who with two other ex-convicts was later able to lease a boat out to the British government as a convict transport? This extraordinary and ironic reversal occurred in 1808 when the business partnership hired out the *Sydney Cove* for transportation.

A few months after the Kables were married they initiated the first civil court case ever held in Australia, in an attempt to claim the parcel of goods charitably donated on their behalf by a sympathetic public back in England. The parcel, £20 of clothes and personal goods, had been loaded aboard the First Fleet, but repeated requests to Captain Duncan Sinclair of the *Alexander* throughout 1788 failed to uncover more than a few books. Since both plaintiffs had signed the marriage register with an X, these books were the least useful goods to them. They claimed that the missing items were worth £15—a sum that would clearly advance the Kables' fortunes beyond many of their fellow convicts. Despite English law which regarded felons (and former felons) as 'already dead in law' and hence unable to sue, the case was allowed to proceed.[3] On 5 July 1788 their writ against the captain of the *Alexander* was heard and the Kables were awarded the full amount they sought.[4]

That two convicts, both still under sentence, were permitted to bring a case to court, to accuse so substantial a personage as a ship's captain and then to win their case was a significant vindication of property rights in a convict society.[5] Would less celebrated convicts have been accorded such access to the law? The very fact that the Kables instigated a court hearing was due to the publicity of their situation and the known interest of high-ranking authorities like the Reverend Richard Johnson, in their well-being. The chaplain of the First Fleet may have been the colonial equivalent of Mr Simpson, the turnkey from Norwich gaol. Johnson was one of three members of the court which judged their case, and he took a particular interest in the Kables, having been entrusted with keeping an eye on the family even before the Fleet sailed. The chaplain, in fact, helped maintain interest at an international level and wrote to the admiralty a week after the court case was heard. He believed that 'the publick seemed to be so much interested in their welfare'.[6]

The financial success of the Kables was not just predicated on the kindness of others, but was also achieved through their own opportunism. Their success as litigants taught them that the law was a powerful ally. It set a precedent for future action in the courts as they pursued other ships' captains as well as business partners and rival traders. In 1807 Governor Bligh claimed that Kable and his partners ruined competitors 'with constant litigation and infamous prosecutions in the Courts'.[7] Although some of Bligh's opinion was generated by personal animosity, it is apparent that Kable followed a ruthless and aggressive course in order to achieve his remarkable success in the colony.

Kable snr also maintained his profile in the settlement by his sheer physical presence. He was a tall, well-built young man whose red hair added yet another point of distinction. Soon after the Fleet's arrival, when Governor Phillip found the marines antagonistic to duties beyond the norm, he was forced to employ the only other manpower available, and a number of convicts were appointed to positions of trust. Henry Kable, who had shown a significant commitment to stable family life and values, was made overseer of the convict women. His own opinion on this posting was: 'I am, thank God, very easily situated, never worked one day since I have been here; some officers have been so pleased with my conduct, that they continue me in the office of an overseer over the women.'[8]

Further authority and freedom followed the Kables throughout the 1790s. Henry snr was appointed as a night watchman, and in 1791 was made a constable. In 1794 the first of a number of land grants came his way; in 1796 he received an absolute pardon and was appointed head constable and gaoler; and in 1797 he was granted a licence to operate an inn in the Rocks area of Sydney and was one of a syndicate of twelve which the governor licensed to build a boat for coastal trading. Throughout this decade Kable amassed sufficient capital for him to diversify into ship-building, sealing and coastal trading. In May 1802 he was dismissed from his government position for misbehaving in the execution of his duty. Nevertheless, his commercial enterprise continued unabated and in February 1810 he leased a brewery from Andrew Thompson.[9] What was the secret of such success?

There was obviously something dynamic in 1790s Sydney which was recognised, seized and exploited by entrepreneurs like Henry Kable. But in this case it was an entrepreneur with a commitment to the colony's future, or at least to a dynastic future—by 1799 seven of the Kables' eleven children had been born. It is this commitment that sets Kable and his associates apart from many of the officer traders concerned only with making a quick fortune and then returning to England. Sydney was rapidly changing, moving from a convict prison to a society immersed in commerce. And to men like Kable it was even more than this: what he recognised was that the colony offered unprecedented chances for families to prosper by yoking their destiny to the colony's future.

At this time the colonial economy was built almost entirely around the government store or commissary: it purchased almost all the grain grown in the colony.[10] Those like Kable who were given early land grants, and who had some vision of a future, grew crops for sale to the commissary. In this way they began to establish a small capital base. Any retail trade outside this was a monopoly controlled by the New South Wales Corps. Kable was able to act as a middleman between these officers and the consumers, and astutely expanded his business sphere of activity. Although initially illiterate, he soon acquired book-keeping and accounting skills. Like other emancipists he became a cuckoo in the nest. David Collins was to comment:

> Not wishing to soil their gentility by too blatant a descent into the market place, they [the officers] permitted the retail trade to fall into the hands of ambitious and able (if uneducated) men with no gentility to lose. By doing so they made affluent those who would oust them from their position of privilege.[11]

By 1800 these officers were not only ousted from their privileged economic position, but most had returned to England. By the turn of the century, trade and commerce in colonial Sydney were firmly in the hands of free merchants or emancipists like Henry Kable. In 1800 Kable formed a partnership with another ex-convict and became one of the founders of the colonial shipbuilding and sealing industries. This was the heyday of the Kable family.

But by 1808 most of Kable's partnerships had been acrimoniously dissolved and a welter of lawsuits followed. Henry Kable jnr, who had been shunted across the English countryside in 1786, now began to play a significant role in his family's affairs. In February 1810 it was reported that Kable jnr, then in his twenties, had 'taken upon himself the entire management of his [father's] Business at Sydney'.[12] This transfer was a safeguard against the lawsuits and when one of these suits went against Kable snr a year later, the well-timed transfer enabled him to avoid paying the staggering sum of £12,000.

Henry Kable snr effectively retired from business at this time, although he was still under fifty. His fortunes in the colony had begun with a successful lawsuit in 1788 and his withdrawal from mainstream business twenty years later was also the result of a similar action, this time against him. He moved to Windsor, forty-odd kilometres from Sydney Cove, where he had substantial land holdings and opened a store and brewery. He lived there for another thirty-five years and died in 1846. Kable Street, Windsor, commemorates this early settler and his descendants today are the second most numerous of any of the First Fleeters.

Because Henry Kable jnr's family was so prominent in the earliest days of settlement and because he was one of the longest-lived children from the First Fleet, it is no wonder that there is more information available on him than on any of his young companions on the voyage. From the very first year of settlement we have two letters that mention this child. They describe Henry jnr as having 'a weakly constitution, but a fine boy' and as a 'promising little fellow'.[13]

As with most of the children of the First Fleet, Henry Kable's birthdate is not at all certain. He was said to be about five months when his mother left Norwich gaol in November 1786 and nine months when the First Fleet set sail. His father described him as already going to school in November 1788 when, according to this chronology, he would have been just over two. Later evidence suggests that the child could have been born as early as 1784—his petition to Governor Brisbane in 1822 stated that he was thirty-eight years old. If his own testimony is to be credited, then in 1788 he would have been a less precocious schoolboy aged four. And yet, to further confuse the issue and show just how conflicting evidence can be, there is the testimony of his headstone. Here the birthdate is 17 February 1786.[14]

Kable jnr was a young child rather than an infant when christened in a joint ceremony with his baby sister Diana or Dinah (born late 1788) at Port Jackson on 5 December 1788. By the end of the century, Henry Kable jnr was one of six surviving children and was to be the eldest of ten. His childhood was spent in Port Jackson and he grew apace with the settlement. Unlike many other founding families, the Kables were not transferred to Norfolk Island or to less distant outposts and remained tied to the developing waterfront town. This stability in their lives enabled them to establish and maintain contacts and to take advantage of increasing colonial opportunities.

Among the many improvements to the Kable family fortunes were a variety of real estate holdings in Sydney. The most significant of these, in domestic terms, was the town block in lower George Street where they built one of the most substantial homes of the day. In 1811, when it was being advertised for lease, the description read:

> convenient and extensive Premises...comprising a commodious Dwelling House, with detached kitchen and out-offices, good stable, large granaries, roomy and substantial store-houses, a Front Retail Warehouse, good cellarage, and every other convenience suited to a commercial house, the whole in complete repair, and unrivalled in point of situation.[15]

Prominent and wealthy emancipists of the time erected their mansions and warehouses along the west side of Sydney Cove to form the first coterie of impressive dwellings in the colony. On either side of the Tank Stream were Lord and Underwood and then progressing down the cove were Kable, Nichols and Reiby.

In 1799, 'being inclined to a seafaring life', Henry Kable jnr joined the crew of the *Rolla* as the master's mate and was not reunited with his family until 1803.[16] Unfortunately, the pleasure of his return was marred when his right arm was severely injured during the launch of one of his father's ships soon after on 21 May 1803:

> On Saturday morning the props were knocked away from under her [the *Governor King*], and she was got down to the water's edge, against the evening tide, when she began to stir, but the pull of the windlass, at which many persons were at work, suddenly giving way, had nearly been productive of the most serious consequences: One of the bars, which flew with incredible force, struck the pilot...Mr. Kable's son, by the sudden recoil, was thrown overboard.'[17]

Despite the limited use of this arm, young Kable continued his seafaring life with voyages to England, America, China and the Pacific Islands. He returned to Sydney in 1807 as a ship's officer and in December 1808 was appointed master of the *Trial*. Two years later the family fortunes had seriously diminished. Most of his father's partnerships had dissolved and the barrage of lawsuits were to continued for the next decade. After Kable snr's transferral of property to his son at the beginning of 1810, Henry jnr formed a shipping partnership with one of his brothers-in-law and continued to captain trading vessels until as late as 1839.[18]

In 1822, this most prosperous child of the First Fleet sought a more settled lifestyle. In the custom of the day he addressed a petition, called a Memorial, to the governor, Sir Thomas Brisbane, seeking 'a Grant of Land, and the requisite Indulgences as allowed to settlers of respectability'.[19] By this time some of his brothers had received similar grants and only the year before an additional 300 acres was added to his father's grants, which had been accumulating since 1803. That this petition, as well as one in September 1824, was refused is less significant than the interpretation it offers of the Kable family history.

One is reminded of the 1787 re-invention of the Kables by the popular press as romantic victims of the system rather than criminals. In 1822 they were again cast as victims. In the words of Kable jnr's petition:

> his aged father being some years ago unfortunately embarrassed in his circumstances in consequence of unavoidable mercantile losses at sea, and at the same time encumbered with a numerous young family; Your Memorialist has resided with him to assist him through his difficulties.[20]

Henry Kable jnr was never as entrepreneurial a figure as his father, as prominent a businessman or as litigious an adversary. Indeed, most of the father's fighting spirit seems to have gone to another son, John Kable (1802–59). He was a noted athlete and strongman and was the first great bare-knuckle fighter in Australia.

Overshadowed by such forthright figures and necessarily limited by his injured right arm, Henry Kable jnr led a less public life. Unlike the rest of his family he never married. It was his sisters, in particular, who were to make advantageous marriages that strengthened and advanced the family fortunes.

This former child of the First Fleet nevertheless established an enviable and illustrious record in the founding years of the colony and his incredible reversal of fortune as an infant ensures him a unique profile in Australia's founding history.

JOHN HUDSON: IN MEMORIAM

> Golden lads and girls all must,
> As chimney-sweepers, come to dust.
>
> Shakespeare, *Cymbeline*, Act IV Scene ii

AFTER tracing less than a decade in the extraordinary life of the child convict John Hudson from the age of nine, it is both sad and unsatisfying to find we can take his story no further. We may prefer to part company with him on a more sanguine note.

Picture him then on a May Day morning in London, on a day traditionally reserved as a holiday for chimneysweeps when they openly cavorted and mocked their audience. This annual event marked a seasonal rite of passage for chimneysweeps. May Day was traditionally the day most families ceased to use fires in their houses and in the warmer seasons many of the mastersweeps would switch over to an even less salubrious occupation—the disposal of night-soil. Their young boys, however, would be turned out onto the streets to beg, to harass the public, to steal.

Mastersweepers in John Hudson's day promoted their services with handbills advertising a range of activities. Although we do not know the name of Hudson's mastersweep, it could easily have been someone like Thomas Crosby. His London handbill was printed the same year that Hudson was convicted. In 1783 Crosby advertised himself as:

> a chimney-sweeper & nightman…acquaint[ing] ladies and gentlemen, that he sweeps chimneys, and cleans smoke stacks, in the best and cheapest manner, having always clean cloaths, and goes with the boys himself…[and] likewise empties bog houses.[1]

These words appear to define the limits of Hudson's choices for the future: nightman or mastersweep. Both jobs would have placed him on the very fringe of society. Unfortunately his choice of petty criminal marginalised him even further and he ended up on the First Fleet.

On May Day Hudson and his young companions burlesqued the repugnant nature of their trade. They capered in the streets and aped what they imagined to be the conventions of polite society. All of this was to the accompaniment of their primitive percussion using the chimney-scrapers and soot-brushes of their trade. They appeared as nothing less than lords of misrule dressed in their pathetic May Day finery. Their clothes were laced with coloured paper and flowers. They wore feathers in their caps and their faces were bedaubed with chalk, meal and red-brick dust. Their shovels were scored with crimson pigment and white chalk and they carried these humble implements of their trade as proudly as any City alderman parading in his finery.

Even without the grotesque decorations they were a race apart. On this day they looked more like a bizarre tribe of natives than young English boys. More like 'a spectacle…better adapted to wild African negroes than to so refined a people as the English'.[2] Indeed, when the First Fleet surgeon George Worgan saw the Australian Aborigines in January 1788 he was reminded of May Day chimneysweeps: 'They [the Aborigines] suffered the sailors to dress them with different colour Papers, and Fools-Caps...the strange contrast these Decorations made with their black Complexion brought to my Mind, the Chimney-Sweeps in London on a May-Day.'[3] Perhaps John Hudson thought of this too when he arrived at Port Jackson.

As part of the May Day celebrations in London, John Hudson may have been one of the lucky boys invited to share in an annual feast. Perhaps he was the guest of Mrs Elizabeth Montagu, queen of the London 'bluestockings' and friend of Dr Samuel Johnson. Mrs Montagu and her friends scorned dancing and card-playing. Rather than pursuing the approved feminine pastimes of the day they chose to rival men in their preference for intelligent conversation and charitable works.

In her undisputed supremacy as hostess to the intellectual society of London, Lady Montagu would entertain the King and Queen and accommodate as many as 700 at breakfast! On this day though, her role, which had become something of a celebrated annual eccentricity, was again to treat London chimneysweeps to traditional English hospitality.[4]

Picture John Hudson not as a skulking burglar in the dead of night, but as an exotic-looking precursor of someone to be sighted at Botany Bay. Instead of witnessing him breaking into a modest dwelling to steal clothing, see him welcomed into the courtyard of a palatial home in Portman Square for a meal of roast meat and plum pudding.

EMIGRATION OF THE SWEEPS—SEEKING OTHER *CLIMES.*

AFTERWORD

A recurring image of handprints and of hands reaching across time generated and inspired much of the writing of this book. John Hudson's sooty handprints were the evidence that sent him to Newgate Prison and earned him a place on the First Fleet. The fact that the child was literally caught by his own hand was a potent aspect in this book's creation.

In the course of researching an earlier book I wondered about the place of children on the First Fleet and the nursery lore they might have brought with them. While I strained to hear those young voices across two hundred years I read Mollie Gillen's *The Founders of Australia*. This book, a milestone in Australian historiography, is a patient and scholarly biographical listing of voyagers on the First Fleet. Here I found a short entry for John Hudson and realised that there were convict children as well as free children on that voyage. These children maintained their presence in my thinking and their voices refused to be silenced.

Not long after, I was fortunate enough to meet Mollie Gillen and a correspondence developed between us. This book owes its very genesis to *The Founders of Australia* and I acknowledge that debt with respect and gratitude.

My greatest hope for this book is that it establishes a place for the children of the First Fleet in our emotions as well as our historical consciousness. I confess that I have sometimes released my own incredulity and anger into writing about what the law did to young offenders like John Hudson; how the state turned its back on these child slaves and how Hudson's childhood was eroded, if not destroyed, by desperation and poverty.

Some readers may prefer their history more measured and remote. My intention has been to convey the pathos these forgotten orphans of 1788 experienced and to give a voice to those who have not been given a speaking part in our historical drama before. My only defence in writing in this way is the simplest one: I could not have written it otherwise.

NOTES

THE INFANT COLONY

Epigraph. Francois Mauriceau, *The Diseases of Women with Child, and in Childbed*, Garland Publishing, New York, 1985, p. 244.

1. Robert Hughes, *The Fatal Shore*, Collins Harvill, London, 1987, p. 74.

2. Two recent and valuable studies of so-called 'juvenile convicts' should be cited. Although they identify a distinct group of convicts hitherto undifferentiated from their adult contemporaries, they disagree on the age limitations of their topic. Their '18 years or under' and '16 years or under' seem to be arbitrarily imposed without any substantiating authority. See Kim Humphery, 'Objects of Compassion: Young Male Convicts in Van Diemen's Land, 1834–1850', in *Australian Historical Studies*, vol. 25 no. 98 (April 1992), pp. 13–33 and Avril Kyle, 'Little Depraved Felons', in *AHS*, vol. 25 no. 99 (October 1992), pp. 319–24.

More ambitious is Portia Robinson's *The Hatch and Brood of Time* (1985) which is a study of the first generation of native-born white Australians. Robinson states, without citing any authority, that '12 years of age and under was the contemporary definition of "children"' (Ch. 1, fn. 2). In 1995 a scholarly work for the Economic History Society published by Cambridge University Press defined children in the period 1780–1890 as 'youngsters under the age of 14' (Pamela Horn, *Children's Work and Welfare, 1780–1890*, p. 3), and Jan Kociumbas's *Australian Childhood* (1997) offers a definition that conforms to eighteenth-century authorities: 'In England, though the criminal law defined young people as children until fourteen, those aged from seven could be held criminally liable if it were proved that they knew they were doing wrong.' (p. 23)

3. Samuel Johnson, *A Dictionary of the English Language*, J. & P. Knapton et al., London, 1755–56. Johnson defines youth as 'The part of life succeeding to childhood and adolescence; the time from fourteen to twenty-eight.' Also William Blackstone, *Commentaries of the Laws of England*, W. Gilbert et al., Dublin, 1788, vol. 4, p. 23. Relevant topics discussed by Blackstone include the mutual duties of parents and children, the legal status of infants, their property rights, the punishment of children, their capacity to act as witnesses and rape by and of children.

4. Mollie Gillen, *The Founders of Australia: A Biographical Dictionary of the First Fleet*, Library of Australian History, Sydney, 1989, p. 41.

5–6. Home Office 42/10, PRO Reel 7184, Henry Bradley to Under Secretary Evan Nepean, 1 November 1786.

7. 'An Address to the Public, from the Philanthropic Society', The Philanthropic Society, London, 1791, p. 26.

8. *Dublin Chronicle*, 1 November 1791 reprinted in *Historical Records of New South Wales*, vol. 2, p. 780.

9. *The Convict's Child*, H. Such, London, c. 1830.

10. *The Gamester*, Cheap Repository for Moral & Religious Tracts, London, [1796], p. 1.

11. Stephen Nicholas & Peter R. Shergold, 'Convicts as Migrants', in *Convict Workers*, S. Nicholas (ed.), CUP, Sydney, 1989, p. 48.

12. *An Account of the Philanthropic Society*, The Philanthropic Society, London, 1797, p. 4.

13. David Collins, *An Account of the English Colony in New South Wales*, A. H. & A. W. Reed, Sydney, 1975, vol. 1, p. 45.

14. Alan Atkinson, *The Europeans in Australia: A History, Volume I: The Beginning*, Oxford University Press, Melbourne, 1998, p. 38.

LONDON 1783

Epigraph. H. Zouch, *Hints Respecting the Public Police*, John Stockdale, London, [1786], p. 2.

1. Henry Fielding, *An Inquiry into the Causes of the Late Increase of Robbers*, A. Millar, London, 1751, p. 3.

2. Tobias Smollett, *Humphrey Clinker*, Penguin Books, Harmondsworth, 1967, p. 118.

3–4. W., 'Sweep, Soot O! or, Some Account of Little Jem, the Chimney Sweeper and His Benefactress', John Marshall, London, c. 1797, pp. 7–8.

5. Charles Lamb, 'In Praise of Chimney-Sweepers: A May-Day Effusion', in *London Magazine*, 1822, vol. 5, p. 405.

6–7. *Old Bailey Session Papers*, no. 1 part 3, 1783, pp. 49–50.

8. Newgate Calendar, 10 December 1783. HO 77/1.

9. L. L. Robson, *The Convict Settlers of Australia*, Melbourne University Press, Carlton, 1976, p. 39.

10. John Howard, *The State of the Prisons in England and Wales, with Preliminary Observations and an Account of Some Foreign Prisons and Hospitals*, William Eyres, Warrington, 1784, 3rd edn, pp. 17–18.

11. *OBSP*, no. 1 part 3, 1783, p. 49.

12. Frank McLynn, *Crime and Punishment in Eighteenth-Century England*, Routledge, London, 1989, p. 87.

13. H. Zouch, op. cit., p. 1.

14–15. *OBSP*, no. 1 part 3, 1783, pp. 49–50.

16. V. A. C. Gatrell, *The Hanging Tree: Execution and the English People 1770–1868*, OUP, Oxford, 1994, pp. 536–37.

17. *OBSP*, no. 1 part 3, 1783, pp. 49–50.

18. William Blackstone, *Commentaries on the Laws of England*, W. Gilbert et al., Dublin, 1788, vol. 4, p. 23.

19–20. *OBSP*, no. 1 part 3, 1783, p. 50.

CHIMNEYSWEEP TO CONVICT

1. Samuel Roberts, 'On the Employment of Climbing Boys', in *The Chimney-Sweeper's Friend, and Climbing-Boy's Album*, James Montgomery (ed.), Longman et al., London, 1824, pp. 13–15.

2. Dr Lushington, 'The Speech of Dr Lushington, in support of the Bill for the Better Regulation of Chimney-Sweepers and their Apprentices, and for Preventing the Employment of Boys in Climbing Chimneys, before the Committee in the House of Lords, on Friday the 13th of March 1818', in James Montgomery (ed.), op. cit., p. 144.

3. *OBSP*, no. 1 part 3, 1783, p. 49.

4. 'An Act for the Better Regulation of Chimney Sweepers', Charles Eyre & Andrew Strahan, London, 1788, p. 437.

5. *OBSP*, no. 1 part 3, 1783, p. 50.

6. Dorothy George, *London Life in the Eighteenth Century*, Penguin, Harmondsworth, 1992, p. 242.

7. *The Times* (London), 25 March 1875, p. 9.

8. Jonas Hanway, *A Sentimental History of Chimney-sweepers*, Dodsley, London, 1785, pp. 79–80.

9. [Twelfth Report] 'Society for Superseding the Necessity of Climbing Boys, by Encouraging a New Method of Sweeping Chimneys, and for Improving the Condition of Children and Others, Employed by Chimney Sweepers', The Society, London, 1827, p. 13.

10. James P. Andrews, *An Appeal to the Humane, on behalf of the Most Deplorable Class of Society, The Climbing Boys, employed by the Chimney-Sweepers*, John Stockdale, London, 1788, p. 8.

11. Jonas Hanway, op. cit., p. 27.

12. David Porter, 'Considerations on the Present State of Chimney Sweepers', David Porter, London, 1801, reprinted in *Improving the Lot of the Chimney Sweeps*

1785–1840, Kenneth Carpenter (ed.), Arno Press, New York, 1972, pp. 35–36.

13. James P. Andrews, op. cit., pp. 16–17.

14. J. L. Hammond & Barbara Hammond, *The Town Labourer*, Longmans, London, 1966, p. 178.

15. James P. Andrews, op. cit., p. 20. See also David Porter, fn. 35 in Kenneth Carpenter, op. cit. Also Henry Earle, 'On Chimney Sweepers' Cancer', in *Medico-Chirurgical Transactions*, 1823, vol. 12 part 2, pp. 296–307.

16–18. Jonas Hanway, op. cit., pp. 27, 14–18 & 44.

19. 'An Act for the Better Regulation of Chimney Sweepers', op. cit., 1788, p. 436.

20. *The Times* (London), 13 March 1819, p. 6.

21. Dorothy George, op. cit., p. 42.

22. Samuel Roberts, 'The Chimney Sweeper's Boy', in James Montgomery, op. cit., pp. 61–62.

23. William Buchan, *Domestic Medicine*, H. Chamberlaine et al., Dublin, 1784, p. 312.

24. William Blake, 'The Chimney Sweeper', in *The Songs of Innocence and Experience*, G. Keynes (ed.), Clarendon Press, Oxford, 1970.

PERCEPTIONS OF CHILDHOOD

1–2. Jonathan Swift, 'A Modest Proposal', in *Jonathan Swift: A Selection of his Works*, Philip Pinkus (ed.), Macmillan, Toronto, 1969, pp. 479–84.

3. William Alexander, *The History of Women*, S. Price et al., Dublin, 1779, vol. 2, p. 266.

4. Jonas Hanway, op. cit., p. 25.

5. Randolph Trumbach, *The Rise of the Egalitarian Family*, Academic Press, New York & London, 1978, p. 262.

6. Reverend J. Howlett, *The Insufficiency of the Causes to Which the Increase of Our Poor, and of the Poor's Rates Have Been Commonly Ascribed*, W. Richardson, London, 1788, pp. 29–30.

7–8. Lawrence Stone, *The Family, Sex and Marriage in England 1500–1800*, Weidenfeld & Nicolson, London, 1977, pp. 470–87.

9. E. P. Thompson, review of Lawrence Stone's *The Family, Sex and Marriage in England, 1500–1800*, in *New Society*, 8 September 1977, p. 501.

10. See Linda Pollock, *Forgotten Children: Parent–Child Relations from 1500 to 1900*,

CUP, Cambridge, 1988; John Gillis, 'Affective Individualism and the English Poor', in *Journal of Interdisciplinary History*, vol. 10 no. 1, 1979, pp. 121–28; and John Scott, 'The History of the Family as an Affective Unit', in *Social History*, 1979, vol. 4 no. 3, pp. 509–16.

11. *The History of Childhood*, Lloyd de Mause (ed.), Souvenir Press, London, 1976, p. 1.

12. Derek Jarrett, *England in the Age of Hogarth*, Yale University Press, New Haven & London, 1974, p. 61.

13. William Cadogan, *An Essay upon Nursing, and the Management of Children, from their Birth to Three Years of Age*, J. Roberts, London, 1748, 2nd edn, p. 14.

14–15. George Armstrong, *An Account of the Diseases Most Incident to Children*, T. Caddell, London, 1783, 4th edn, pp. 5–6.

16. Frederick Morton Eden, *The State of the Poor, or, An History of the Labouring Classes in England*, B. & J. White et al., London, 1797, vol. 1, pp. 449–50.

17. Quoted in Dorothy George, op. cit., p. 56.

18. James Stephen Taylor, *Jonas Hanway, Founder of the Marine Society: Charity and Policy in Eighteenth-Century Britain*, Scolar Press, London & Berkeley, 1985, p. 188.

19–20. Frederick Morton Eden, op. cit., vol. 1, pp. 298–99.

21. John Moir, *Female Tuition; or, An Address to Mothers on the Education of Daughters*, J. Murray, Dublin, 1787, p. 182.

22. George Rosen, 'A Slaughter of Innocents: Aspects of Child Health in the Eighteenth-Century City', in *Studies in Eighteenth-Century Culture*, vol. 5, 1976, p. 302.

23. J. Scott & L. Tilley, 'Women's Work and the Family in Nineteenth-Century Europe', in *Comparative Studies in Society and History*, vol. 17 no. 1, 1975, p. 42.

24. Jonas Hanway, *A Comprehensive View of Sunday Schools with Reflections on the Causes of the Decay of our Morals and National Piety*, Dodsley, London, 1786, pp. i–ii.

25. Derek Jarrett, op. cit., p. 79.

26. Quoted in Michael Rosen, *The Penguin Book of Childhood*, Viking, London, 1994, p. 44.

27. Jonas Hanway, *Observations of the Causes of the Dissoluteness Which Reigns Among the Lower Classes of the People*, Marine Society, London, 1772, p. 37.

28. J. P. Grosley, *A Tour in London, 1772*, quoted in Leon Radzinowicz, *A History of English Criminal Law and Its Administration Since 1750*, Steven & Sons, London, 1948–1986, vol. 1, p. 176, fn. 50.

29. *OBSP*, no. 1 part 3, 1783, p. 50.

30. John Styles, 'Sir John Fielding and the Problem of Criminal Investigation in Eighteenth-Century England', in *Transactions of the Royal Historical Society*, 5th series no. 33, 1983, pp. 127–49.

31. *OBSP*, no. 1 part 2, 1783, p. 49.

NEWGATE PRISON—AN ENTRANCE TO HELL

1. 'Report of the Committee of the Society for the Improvement of Prison Discipline, and for the Reformation of Juvenile Offenders', The Philanthropic Society, London, 1818, p. 24.

2. John Howard, op. cit., 1777, p. 16.

3. W. J. Sheehan, 'Finding Solace in Eighteenth-Century Newgate', in *Crime in England 1550–1800*, J. S. Cockburn (ed.), Princeton University Press, Princeton, 1977, p. 236.

4. William Smith, *The State of the Gaols in London, Westminster, and the Borough of Southwark*, J. Bew, London, 1776, pp. 9–10.

5. W. J. Sheehan, op. cit., pp. 229–45.

6. Daniel Defoe, *The Fortunes and Misfortunes of the Famous Moll Flanders* [1722], Penguin, Harmondsworth, 1972, p. 300.

7. HO 42/6, PRO Reel 7194, January 1785. 'Report [of] The Committee appointed to Enquire What Proceedings Have Been Had in the Execution of an Act for the Effectual Transportation of Felons', p. 453.

A NURSERY OF CRIME

Epigraph. 'Report of the Committee of the Society for the Improvement of Prison Discipline, and for the Reformation of Juvenile Offenders', op. cit., p. 24.

1. Ibid, 1820, p. xxv.

2. John Howard, *The State of the Prisons in England and Wales, with Preliminary Observations and an Account of Some Foreign Prisons and Hospitals*, William Eyres, Warrington, 1784, 3rd edn, p. 213.

3. Josiah Dornford, *Nine Letters to the Right Honourable the Lord Mayor and Aldermen of the City of London, on the State of the City Prisons and Prisoners within their Jurisdiction*, Josiah Dornford, London, 1786, p. 14.

4. 'Report of the Committee of the Society for the Improvement of Prison Discipline, and for the Reformation of Juvenile Offenders', op. cit., 1818, pp. 18–19, p. 24.

5. John Howard, op. cit., 1784, p. 213.

6. Josiah Dornford, op. cit., p. 34.

7. 'Copy of a Despatch from Earl Grey to Lieutenant-Governor Sir William Denison', 30 September 1846, in *British Parliamentary Papers: Correspondence and Papers Relating to Convict Ships, Convict Discipline and Transportation 1843–47*, Irish University Press, Shannon, 1969, vol. 7, pp. 521–22.

8. *HRNSW*, vol. 1 part 2, [February? 1787], pp. 50–51.

9–10. Tobias Smollett, op. cit., p. 118.

11. Jonas Hanway, *The Neglect of the Effectual Separation of Prisoners, and the Want of Good Order and Religious Oeconomy in Our Prisons*, Jonas Hanway, London, 1784, p. 9.

12. *OBSP*, July 1784, p. 874.

13. Quoted in John Cobley, *The Crimes of the First Fleet*, Angus & Robertson, Sydney, 1970, p. xi.

14. Adm. 1/4151, PRO Reel 5884, letter from Lord Sydney to the admiralty, 29 May 1784.

15. John Howard, op. cit., 1784, p. 382.

16–17. Quoted in Mollie Gillen, 'His Majesty's Mercy: The Circumstances of the First Fleet', in *Push*, no. 29, 1991, pp. 94–95.

18. HO 13/6, PRO Reel 655, Under Secretary Evan Nepean to the mayor and the recorder of the City of Chester, in a footnote, 12 December 1787.

19. Quoted in Mollie Gillen, 'His Majesty's Mercy', op. cit., p. 97.

20. Adm. 1/4151, PRO Reel 5884, John P. Bastard to Lord Sydney in a letter, 5 November 1784.

21. Quoted in Mollie Gillen, 'His Majesty's Mercy', op. cit., p. 97.

22. 'Account of Cloathing issued to the Convicts on Board his Majesty's Ship *Dunkirk* at Plymouth by William Cowdry', T1/613, PRO Reel 3549.

23. Quoted in Mollie Gillen, *The Search for John Small, First Fleeter*, Library of Australian History, Sydney, 1988, p. 70.

24. HO 42/8, PRO Reel 7194, William Cowdry to Navy Board, 11 March 1786.

25. HO 42/8, PRO Reel 7194, William Cowdry to Navy Board, 17 March 1786.

26–27. T1/692, PRO Reel 3551, sworn statement from John Groundwater, deputy overseer of the *Dunkirk* from March 1786 to March 1791.

28. T1/692, PRO Reel 3551, Dr Richardson's statement.

29. Quoted in Mollie Gillen, *The Founders of Australia*, op. cit., p. 402.

30. 'List of the Members of the Philanthropic Society', Philanthropic Press, London, 1791, p. 1.

31. 'Account of the Nature and Views of the Philanthropic Society for the Prevention of Crimes, by the Admission of the Offspring of Convicts, and for the Reform of Criminal Poor Children', The Philanthropic Society, London, 1799, p. 18.

32. Ibid, 1797, p. 5.

33. 'The Philanthropic Society, Instituted September 1788 for the Prevention of Crimes, and the Reform of the Criminal Poor by the Encouragement of Industry, and the Culture of Good Morals, among those Children Who Are Now Training Up to Vicious Courses, Public Plunder, Infamy and Ruin', The Society, London, 1790, p. 17; and 'Account of the Nature and Views of the Philanthropic Society for the Prevention of Crimes, by the Admission of the Offspring of Convicts, and for the Reform of Criminal Poor Children', op. cit., 1797, pp. 18–19.

A CELEBRATED FIRST FLEET FAMILY

Epigraph. Watkin Tench, *Sydney's First Four Years*, Angus & Robertson, Sydney, 1961, p. 12.

1. Susannah Holmes, Elizabeth Pulley and Ann Turner.

2. Simpson arrived at Plymouth on 5 November 1786.

3. Yet Edward Parkinson, aged two, arrived on the *Dunkirk* on 1 November 1786 and Ann and William Smith, both one, embarked the following month.

4. They were not married until 10 February 1788.

5. John Simpson received fifteen guineas from titled admirers and was subsequently appointed as an officer of the Norwich sheriff's court. See *Daily Universal Register*, 21 December 1786, p. 3.

6. 'Narrative relating to a Convict Ordered to be Transported to Botany Bay', from *Scot's Magazine*, vol. 48, November 1786, reprinted in *Freedom Bound I: Documents on Women in Colonial Australia*, Marian Quartly et al. (eds), Allen & Unwin, Sydney, 1995, pp. 6–9.

7. The entire story was reprinted in the *London Chronicle*, 2–5 December 1786, p. 539. It also appeared in the *Norfolk Chronicle* over four issues: 11 November, 9 December, 23 December 1786 and 6 January 1787. See also the *Gentleman's Magazine* (London) supplement for the year 1786, pp. 1138–40.

8. Daniel Defoe, *Voyage Round the World*, F. Noble, London, 1787, vol. 3, pp. 246–57.

9. Reverend Richard Johnson to Evan Nepean, 12 July 1788, *HRNSW*, vol. 1 part 2, p. 181.

10. Henry Kable to Dinah Cable, *London Chronicle*, 23 July 1789.

11. *Norfolk Chronicle*, 11 November 1786.

12. Quoted in Mollie Gillen, *The Founders of Australia*, op. cit., p. 178.

13. *The Times* (London), 15 December 1786.

A FLOATING NURSERY

1–3. Arthur Bowes Smyth, *The Journal of Arthur Bowes Smyth: Surgeon, Lady Penrhyn, 1787–1789*, Australian Documents Library, Sydney, 1979: 31 May 1787, p. 18; 1 December 1787, p. 46; 18 December 1787, p. 49; 1 December 1787, p. 45.

4–5. George Armstrong [1767], *An Account of the Diseases Most Incident to Children*, T. Caddell, London, 1783, 4th edn, pp. 196–97.

6. Sarah Trimmer, 'The Oeconomy of Charity, Or, An Address to Ladies concerning Sunday-schools', T. Longman et al., London, 1787, pp. 93–94.

7. William Cadogan, 'An Essay upon Nursing, and the Management of Children, from their Birth to Three Years of Age', J. Roberts, London, 1748, 2nd edn, p. 7.

8. Ruth Perry, 'Colonizing the Breast: Sexuality and Maternity in Eighteenth-Century England', in *Forbidden History: The State, Society, and the Regulation of Sexuality in Modern Europe*, John C. Fout (ed.), University of Chicago Press, Chicago, 1992, p. 116.

9–10. George Armstrong, op. cit., pp. 5–6, p. 116.

11. John White, *Journal of a Voyage to New South Wales*, Angus & Robertson, Sydney, 1962, [14 October 1787] p. 90.

12. Arthur Bowes Smyth, op. cit., 13 October 1787, p. 40.

13. Dr Hamilton, professor of Midwifery, Edinburgh, and author of *Treatise on Midwifery* [1781], as quoted in *With Child: Birth through the Ages*, Jenny Carter & Therese Duriez (eds), Mainstream Publishing, Edinburgh, 1986, p. 20.

14. Jan Kociumbas, *Australian Childhood: A History*, Allen & Unwin, Sydney, 1997, p. 5.

15. Quoted in Mollie Gillen, *The Founders of Australia*, op. cit., p. 212.

16. John White, op. cit., 23 June 1787, p. 63.

17. Paul-Gabriel Bouce, 'Some Sexual Beliefs and Myths in Eighteenth-Century Britain', in *Sexuality in Eighteenth-Century Britain*, Paul-Gabriel Bouce (ed.), Manchester University Press, Manchester, 1982, pp. 28–46; Paul-Gabriel

Bouce, 'Imagination, Pregnant Women and Monsters in Eighteenth-Century England and France', in *Sexual Underworlds of the Enlightenment*, G. S. Rousseau & Roy Porter (eds), Manchester University Press, Manchester, 1987, pp. 86–100; Roy Porter, 'Mixed Feelings: The Enlightenment and Sexuality in Eighteenth-Century Britain', in *Sexuality in Eighteenth-Century Britain*, pp. 1–27.

18. Adrian Wilson, *The Making of Man—Midwifery: Childbirth in England 1660–1770*, UCL Press, London, 1995, p. 200.

19–20. Dr Buchan quoted in Adrian Wilson, op. cit., p. 203.

21. CO 201/3, PRO Reel 1, 12 July 1788.

22. T1/667, PRO Reel 3551, Lord Sydney to Treasury, 24 April 1789.

23. CO 201/5, PRO Reel 1, Second Fleet ship, *Neptune*, 17 November 1789.

24. Arthur Bowes Smyth, op. cit., 10 December 1787, p. 48.

25. Sir John Fitzpatrick to A. Graham, 26 January 1802, *Historical Records of Australia*, series 1 vol. 3, p. 372.

26. Sarah Smith's 1825 Memorial, Archives Office NSW 4/1840C, 777. In this memorial Smith claimed she had come free to the colony in 1790 'together with six other females sent out by Government for the purpose of practising midwifery per ship *Neptune*'. It is true that she became a valued midwife in the colony, though her claim seems quite unsubstantiated. See Michael Flynn, *The Second Fleet: Britain's Grim Convict Armada of 1790*, Library of Australian History, Sydney, 1993, pp. 541–42.

27. Arthur Bowes Smyth, op. cit., 5 July 1787, p. 24.

28–29. Thomas Denman, *Introduction to the Practice of Midwifery*, Thomas Denman, London, 1782, p. 58, p. 155.

30. Quoted in B. Hamilton, 'The Medical Professions in the Eighteenth Century', in *Economic History Review*, 2nd series vol. 4 (1951), p. 151.

31. James Nelson, *An Essay on the Government of Children*, R. & J. Dodsley, London, 1753, pp. 44–45.

32. Michael Underwood, *Treatise on the Diseases of Children*, J. Mathews, London, 1784, vol. 3, p. 215.

33. *Women As Mothers in Pre-Industrial England*, Valerie Fildes (ed.), Routledge, London, 1990, p. 86.

34. Letter from an officer on board the *Scarborough*, *HRNSW*, vol. 2, November 1787, p. 740.

VOYAGE AND LANDFALL

1. Quoted in Russell Dobash, *The Imprisonment of Women*, Blackwell, Oxford, 1986, p. 45.

2. Sir Richard Philips, a sheriff of the City of London, in 1808, quoted in J. Tobias, *Prince of Fences: The Life and Crimes of Ikey Solomons*, Ballantine, Mitchell, London, 1974, p. 65.

3–5. Arthur Bowes Smyth, op. cit.: 28 April 1787, p. 14; 1 July 1787, p. 22; 24 September 1787, p. 38 and 31 December 1787, p. 52.

6–7. Thrasycles Clarke, 'Journal of Female Convict Ship *Kains* 1830–31— General Remarks', n. p., Adm 101/40, PRO Reel 3199.

8. Governor Phillip to Under Secretary Evan Nepean, 18 March 1787, *HRNSW*, vol. 1 part 2, p. 59.

9. Lords of admiralty to Lord Sydney, 21 November 1786, *HRNSW*, vol. 1 part 2, p. 29.

10. Major Ross to Secretary Stephens, 13 April 1787, *HRNSW*, vol. 2, p. 78.

11. Major Ross to Under Secretary Evan Nepean, 27 April 1787, *HRNSW*, vol 1 part 2, p. 93.

12. Captain Phillip to Under Secretary Evan Nepean, 18 March 1787, *HRNSW*, vol. 1 part 2, p. 58.

13. Ian Cameron, *Lost Paradise: The Exploration of the Pacific*, Salem House, Topsfield, 1987, p. 14.

14. Barron Field, 'The Kangaroo', in *First Fruits of Australian Poetry*, Barn on the Hill, Sydney, 1941, p. 9.

THE INFANT COLONY CHRISTENED

Epigraph. 'A convict's letter', 9 April 1790, *HRNSW*, vol. 2, pp. 758–59.

1. Watkin Tench, op. cit., p. 36.

2. H. Luson, *Inferior Politics: Or, Considerations on the State of the Poor*, H. Luson, London, 1788, p. 5.

3. Lieutenant Philip Gidley King, *The Journal of Philip Gidley King: Lieutenant, R. N. 1787–1790*, Paul G. Fidlon (ed.), 20 January 1788, Australian Documents Library, 1980, Sydney, p. 35.

4. George Worgan, *Journal of a First Fleet Surgeon*, Library Council New South Wales, Sydney, 1978, p. 4.

5. *HRA*, series 1 vol. 2, p. 488.

6. James Scott, 'Remarks on a Passage to Botany Bay, 1787–1792', 26 January 1788, Public Library NSW, Sydney, 1963, p. 35.

7. Arthur Bowes Smyth, op. cit., 6 February 1788, p. 67.

8. Lieutenant Ralph Clark, *The Journal and Letters of Lt. Ralph Clark 1787–1792*, Australian Documents Library, Sydney, 1981, 11 February 1788.

9. Arthur Bowes Smyth, op. cit., 6 February 1788, p. 67.

10. Judith Cook, *To Brave Every Danger: The Epic Life of Highwaywoman Mary Bryant*, Pan Books, London, 1994, p. 102.

11. Marian Aveling, 'Gender in Early New South Wales Society', in *The Push from the Bush*, no. 24, April 1987, p. 31.

12. Watkin Tench, op. cit., p. 39.

13. Robert Hughes, op. cit., pp. 88–89.

14. Alan Frost, *Botany Bay Mirages: Illusions of Australia's Convict Beginnings*, MUP, Carlton, 1994, p. 168.

15. Quoted in Peter Kemp, *The British Sailor: A Social History of the Lower Deck*, J. M. Dent & Sons, London, 1970, p. 169.

16. Ralph Clark, op. cit., 7 February 1788, p. 96.

17. David Collins, quoted in Alan Atkinson, op. cit., p. 88.

18. William Crook, letter to a friend in England from Parramatta, 31 December 1804, quoted in Portia Robinson, *The Hatch and Brood of Time: A Study of the First Generation of Native-born White Australians 1788–1828*, MUP, Carlton, 1985, p. 23.

19. Surgeon's mate John Lowes, letter to the *Dublin Chronicle* published 13 January 1791, reprinted in *HRNSW*, vol. 2, pp. 770–71.

20. Watkin Tench, op. cit., late 1788, p. 137.

21. Quoted in Mollie Gillen, *The Founders of Australia*, op. cit., p. 169.

22. 'A convict's letter', 9 April 1790, *HRNSW*, vol. 2, pp. 758–59.

23. George Worgan, op. cit., 28 May 1788, p. 49.

NORFOLK ISLAND

Epigraph. Lieutenant Ralph Clark, op. cit., 14 March 1790, p. 120.

1. Quoted by Surgeon John White to Mr Skill in a letter, 17 April 1790, *HRNSW*, vol. 1 part 2, p.333.

2. Governor Phillip's instructions, 25 April 1787, *HRA*, vol. 1 series 1, p. 13.

3. David Collins, op. cit., vol. 1, p. 45.

4. Governor Phillip to Lord Sydney, 11 April 1790, *HRNSW*, vol. 1 part 2, p. 35.

5. HMS *Sirius* muster March–April 1790: marines embarked 4 March 1790 Port Jackson for Norfolk Island, Adm. 36/10978. This document also lists convicts and convict children.

6–8. Lieutenant Ralph Clark, op. cit., 6 March 1790, p. 117.

9. Ibid, 13 March 1790, p. 119.

10. Newton Fowell, letter no. 20 dated 31 July 1790 in *The Sirius Letters*, Nance Irvine (ed.), Fairfax Library, Sydney, 1988, p. 120.

11. Lieutenant-Governor Ross, Proclamation, 20 March 1790, *HRNSW*, vol. 1 part 2, p. 323.

12. Lieutenant-Governor Ross, Proclamation, 7 August 1790, *HRNSW*, vol. 1 part 2, p. 393.

13. Ralph Clark, op. cit., 30 April 1790, p. 130.

14. Lieutenant-Governor Ross, General Order, 8 January 1791, *HRA*, vol. 1 series 1, p. 243.

15. Governor Ross to Governor Phillip, 11 February 1791, *HRA*, vol. 1 series 1, p. 234.

16. Governor King to Governor Phillip, 19 September 1792, *HRA*, vol. 1 series 1, p. 386.

17. Mollie Gillen, *The Founders of Australia*, op. cit., p. 315.

18. John Harris, 20 March 1791, Mitchell Library Ms A1 597, p. 12.

19–21. Ralph Clark, op. cit.: 15 February 1791, p. 183; 20 October 1791, p. 218; 9 April 1791, p. 192.

22. Lieutenant King to Evan Nepean, 23 November 1791, *HRNSW*, vol. 1 part 2, p. 562.

23. Susannah Hunt (c.1748–1814) arrived at Norfolk Island in August 1790 as the schoolteacher. From 1796 she began to benefit from an annual grant from the Society for the Propagation of the Gospel in recognition of her work. Her husband, William Mitchell, a First Fleet seaman, was overseer of the orphan school. (David Collins, op. cit., vol. 1, pp. 423 & 609.)

24. Ibid, p. 609 fn. 7.

25. Alexander MacConichie, 'Observations on Report Regarding the Present State of Norfolk Island', reprinted in *British Parliamentary Papers: Correspondence and Papers Relating to Convict Ships 1843–47*, Irish University Press, Shannon, Ireland, 1969, vol. 7, p. 561.

26. Reverend T. B. Naylor, 'Extract of a Paper Addressed to Lord Stanley', reprinted in *British Parliamentary Papers: Correspondence and Papers Relating to Convict Ships 1843–47*, vol. 7, p. 525.

27. R. Stewart, 'Copy of a Report…to the Comptroller-General', reprinted in *British Parliamentary Papers: Correspondence and Papers relating to Convict Ships 1843–47*, vol. 7, p. 542.

28. *OBSP*, no. 1 part 3, 1783, p. 50.

THE DEVIL AT BOTANY BAY

1. David Collins, *An Account of the English Colony in New South Wales*, op. cit., p. 66.

2–5. Court of Criminal Jurisdiction, Minutes of Proceedings, 1789, Archives Office NSW Reel 2391, 5/1147A, pp. 141–42.

6–10. Ibid, pp. 142–47.

11. David Collins, op. cit., p. 66.

12. Ralph Clark, op. cit., 17 November 1791, p. 224.

13–26. Court of Criminal Jurisdiction, Minutes of Proceedings, 9–10 August 1796, Archives Office NSW Reel 2391, 5/1147B, pp. 155–63.

27–28. Quoted in Michael Flynn, op. cit., p. 347.

29. *Sydney Gazette*, 18 August 1805, p. 1.

FAMILY BLESSINGS

Epigraph. S. T. Coleridge, 'The Delinquent Travellers', in *The Complete Poetical Works*, E. H. Coleridge (ed.), Clarendon Press, Oxford, 1912, vol. 1, p. 446.

1. See Belinda Meteyard, 'Illegitimacy and Marriage in Eighteenth-Century England', in *Journal of Interdisciplinary History*, vol. 10 no. 3, 1980, pp. 479–89; Louise A. Tilley et al., 'Women's Work and European Fertility Patterns', in *Journal of Interdisciplinary History*, vol. 6, 1976, pp. 447–76.

2. John Hunter, *Governor Hunter's Remarks on the Causes of the Colonial Expense of the Establishment of New South Wales etc., Hints for the Reduction of Such Expense, and for Reforming the Prevailing Abuses*, S. Gosnell, London, 1802, p. 30.

3. William Blackstone quoted in David Neal, *The Rule of Law in a Penal Colony: Law and Power in Early New South Wales*, CUP, Cambridge, 1991, p. 6.

4. Archives Office of New South Wales, Court of Civil Jurisdiction, Rough Minutes of Proceedings, vol. 1, 1788, Reel 2391, 5/1147A, pp. 1–8.

5. David Neal, op. cit., pp. 5–7.

6. Reverend Richard Johnson to Evan Nepean, 12 July 1788, *HRNSW*, vol. 1 part 2, p. 181.

7. William Bligh to W. Windham, 31 October 1807, Banks Papers, Mitchell Library, State Library of New South Wales, A85, p. 225.

8. Henry Kable to Dinah Cable, *London Chronicle*, 21–23 July 1789, p. 77.

9. See David R. Hainsworth, *The Sydney Traders: Simeon Lord and his Contemporaries 1788–1821*, MUP, Carlton, 1981; the *Australian Dictionary of Biography*; and, less reliably, *Australian Biographical and Genealogical Record*, John T. Spurway (ed.), ABGR, Sydney, 1992.

10. See N. G. Butlin, *Free Lunches Antipodean Style: NSW Economy 1788–1810*, Australian National University, Canberra, 1985; Lynne McLoughlin, 'Landed Peasantry or Landed Gentry: A Geography of Land Grants', in *A Difficult Infant: Sydney before Macquarie*, Graeme Aplin (ed.), UNSW Press, Sydney, 1988, pp. 120–47.

11. Quoted in D. R. Hainsworth, op. cit., p. 41.

12. *Sydney Gazette*, 11 February 1810, p. 2.

13. Reverend Johnson to Evan Nepean, 12 July 1788, *HRNSW*, vol. 1 part 2, p. 181; Henry Kable to Dinah Cable, *London Chronicle*, 21–23 July 1789, p. 77.

14. *Truth* (Sydney), 'Old Sydney', 8 July 1917, p. 12.

15. *Sydney Gazette*, 6 April 1811, p. 4.

16. Archives Office of New South Wales, Memorial 4/1838 (1822).

17. *Sydney Gazette*, 29 May 1803, p. 3.

18. *Australian*, 14 February 1839, p. 2.

19–20. Archives Office of New South Wales, Memorial 4/1838 (1822).

JOHN HUDSON: IN MEMORIAM

1. Thomas Crosby, single sheet handbill, London, n. p., 1783, from the Royal College of Arts Library, London, ESTCT 218801.

2. Robert Southey, *Letters from England*, Longman et al., London, 1806, 2nd edn, vol. 1, Letter XIII, 4 May 1802, p. 143.

3. George Worgan, op. cit., p. 3.

4. George L. Phillips, 'Mrs Montagu and the Climbing Boys', in *Review of English Studies*, vol. 24, 1948, pp. 237–244; Charles Phythian-Adams, 'Milk and Soot: The Changing Vocabulary of a Popular Ritual in Stuart and Hanoverian London', in *The Pursuit of Urban History*, Derek Fraser (ed.), Edward Arnold, London, 1983, pp. 83–104.

A BIOGRAPHICAL INDEX
OF THE CHILDREN
OF THE FIRST FLEET

Primarily compiled from Mollie Gillen's *The Founders of Australia*; 1787 Victualling List for Teneriffe, Rio de Janeiro & Cape of Good Hope (T46/22, PRO Reel 1106); 1788 Victualling List for Port Jackson (T1/668, PRO Reel 3551); Log of *Lady Penrhyn* (Adm. 51/4376, PRO Reel 5777); St. Phillip's Register of Baptisms (Mitchell Library Mss D 362).

ABEL, William (1787–1788)

William Abel was the son of convict Mary Abel. He was conceived in Worcester gaol where his mother was held from early 1785 to late 1786. The child was born on the *Lady Penrhyn* on 13 April 1787—exactly one month before the Fleet sailed. The surgeon, Arthur Bowes Smyth, described the child as 'a Boy who is likely to do very well'. William Abel was christened on 20 April 1787. His mother married the convict Thomas Tilley on 4 May 1788. William died at Port Jackson later that month, on 19 May, and his mother two months later.

ABRAHAMS, Esther/Rosanna (1787–1837)

Esther Abrahams was born in Newgate Prison to a convict mother of the same name on 18 March 1787. Her mother was only just pregnant when caught for theft on 27 July 1786. She was sentenced to seven years' transportation on 30 August 1786. On 30 April 1787 mother and daughter were among a last-minute round-up of thirty-eight convict women sent to the First Fleet. They travelled by wagon to Portsmouth and embarked on the *Prince of Wales* on 3 May. Both were soon transferred to the *Lady Penrhyn* where the striking young mother caught the eye of First Lieutenant George Johnston.

Esther Abrahams junior was ten months old when she arrived in Port Jackson. On 4 March 1790 the child, her mother and her baby brother George (by Lieutenant Johnston) went to Norfolk Island on the *Sirius*. She was one of five children from the First Fleet with a convict mother who went on this vessel. Just over a year later, on 14 May 1791, Esther junior and her family returned to Port Jackson. The child's mother did not marry Johnston until 1814 and their daughter Blanche (c.1806–1904) is sometimes cited as the longest-lived child of the First Fleeters. (Another contender for this distinction was Sarah Nicholls, c.1823–1907, daughter and last child of First Fleet convict John Nicholls.)

On 18 February 1805, aged eighteen, the young Esther, as Rosanna Julian—Julian was a surname used by both mother and daughter—married a former convict from the Third Fleet, Isaac Nichols. Nichols was the first postmaster in the colony and later became superintendent of convicts. As the second wife of a respected and prosperous member of the community, Esther was hostess in a grand house in the Rocks.

She bore three sons to Nichols (1807–1811) before her husband's death in 1819. Her second son, George Nichols (1809–1857) had an outstanding legal career in the colony, was editor and part owner of the *Australian* newspaper, was elected to the New South Wales Legislative Council in 1848 and served as the colony's first auditor-general. The year after her first husband's death Esther married James Stewart (Stuart). She died on 11 April 1837, aged forty-nine. (See Memorial, CSIL 4/1822, no.167, Archives Office NSW.)

BACON, Elizabeth (c.1788–?)

Elizabeth Bacon was the daughter of marine private Samuel Bacon and his wife Jane. The couple embarked at Plymouth on the *Charlotte* on 10 March 1787. On 21 March they were transferred to the *Sirius* and made the remainder of the voyage on this vessel. Elizabeth is not listed on any of the three Victualling Lists and was presumably born after the Fleet left the Cape of Good Hope (post 11 November 1787). She was christened on 10 February 1788 at Port Jackson.

On 13 December 1791, when Elizabeth Bacon was almost four years old, she left the colony on the *Gorgon* to return to England with her parents. Her twin baby brothers, who had been born in the colony, died on this return voyage. Elizabeth's life thereafter is unrecorded.

BAGLEY, Maria (?–?)

Maria Bagley was the daughter of Ralph Bagley, a marine corporal and his wife Sarah. It is not known which ship the family embarked on. The fact that they embarked at Plymouth on 10 March 1787, however, almost certainly means that they travelled on the *Charlotte*. The family returned to England on the *Gorgon*, leaving the colony on 13 December 1791.

BAUGHAN/BINGHAM/BUNHAM, James/John (1787–1788)

This child is the most elusive of those on the First Fleet. As John Bunham his birth is recorded by Surgeon Bowes Smyth, probably on the *Charlotte*. This is his only mention—his name does not appear on any of the three Victualling Lists or in the logs of any of the transports. He was most likely the child of convict parents, John Baughan and Mary Cleaver, who had met on the *Dunkirk* some time between late 1786 and early 1787. The couple married on

17 February 1788 and a James Baughan was christened on 27 March 1788 (see St Phillip's Register). The child died the very next day.

BELLAMY, Joseph. See DOWNEY, Joseph.

BENTLEY/MORTON/MOULTON, Joshua (1787–1790)

Joshua Bentley was the son of a seaman of the same name and a convict mother, almost certainly Mary Ann Morton/Moulton. The child was born on the *Lady Penrhyn* on 15 November 1787. (The ship's log on that date credits Ann Moulton with a daughter.) The St Phillip's Register lists Joshua Bentley as christened at Port Jackson on 21 January 1788. Surely this is the first christening in Australia? The boy survived until 14 February 1790.

BINGHAM, James. See BAUGHAN, James.

BOLTON/BOULTON, Rebecca (1786–1788)

Rebecca Bolton was the daughter of a convict mother of the same name. The child was conceived in Lincoln gaol and born around April 1786. On 30 December that year the gaoler in Spilsby, Lincolnshire, wrote to the authorities seeking permission for the mother to take her child onto the First Fleet. He wrote 'she has a Female Child about 8 months old, should be glad you'd inform me Wether the child can go with the Mother, she being very desirous to take it'. Permission was granted on 22 March 1787, just in time to keep mother and daughter together (see PRO 419).

The pair boarded the *Prince of Wales* one week later on 28 March 1787 (see ship's log ADM 51/4376, PRO 5777). They disembarked at Port Jackson on 6 February 1788. The mother died on 21 April that year and the child survived her by only one week, dying herself on 28 April.

BRAUND/BRYANT, Charlotte. See SPENCE, Charlotte.

BUNHAM, James. See BAUGHAN, James.

CABELL/CABLE, Henry. See KABLE, Henry.

CAMPBELL, James Duncan (c.1779–?)

James Campbell was the nephew of Captain Campbell (see Bowes Smyth's Journal, p. 15) and sailed on the *Lady Penrhyn*. His uncle was one of four company commanders and second-in-command to Major Ross. The young boy was the only possible friend and peer of young Alexander Ross (qv). James Campbell left Port Jackson on the *Gorgon* on 13 December 1791 for England and was listed as a marine volunteer.

CHAPMAN, Elizabeth (c.1781–?)

Elizabeth Chapman was one of two daughters of Thomas Chapman, corporal of marines, and his wife Jane. The child accompanied her parents and sister Jane Chapman (qv) onto the *Prince of Wales* at the beginning of April 1787. On 23 August 1789 she was raped at Port Jackson by a marine, Henry Wright and on 10 September her case went to court. She returned to England with her family on the *Gorgon*, leaving the colony on 13 December 1791.

CHAPMAN, Jane (178?–?)

Jane Chapman was one of two daughters of Thomas and Jane Chapman. The child accompanied her parents and sister Elizabeth Chapman (qv) onto the *Prince of Wales* at the beginning of April 1787. She returned to England with her family on the *Gorgon*, leaving the colony on 13 December 1791.

CHARLICUT, Mary Ann. See WRIGHT, Mary Ann.

CLEMENT/DALTON/DUTTON, Francis Hannah (1788–1800)

Francis Hannah Clement is thought to be the daughter of the convict Elizabeth Dalton alias Burleigh/Burley, and the seaman (actually ship's carpenter) John Clement. She was probably born in the week before the *Lady Penrhyn* disembarked and was entered on the 1788 Victualling List on 5 April 1788 as Francis Dutton. Two weeks later, on 20 April 1788, she was christened as Francis Hannah Clement (see St Phillip's Register). She died (or was buried) on 23 January 1800 aged eleven.

Although precise dates and details remain uncertain, Francis Hannah Clement is now considered the first white child born in Australia.

COLETHREAD/COULTHREAD, James (c.1782–?)

James Colethread was the young son of a marine private John Colethread and travelled with his father on the *Lady Penrhyn*. There is no record to indicate that the child's mother accompanied the pair.

COLLEY, William (1787)

Elizabeth Colley, convict, gave birth to a stillborn son on the *Lady Penrhyn* on 4 July 1787.

COLLPITTS, William (1787)

Ann Collpitts, convict, gave birth to a son in 1787 on the *Lady Penrhyn*. There is much uncertainty about this child—there is no record of his presence in the fleet nor of his baptism or death in the colony. For these reasons we assume that he was stillborn.

COULTHREAD, James. See COLETHREAD, James.

COX, Joseph. See GOUGH, Joseph.

DALTON, Francis Hannah. See CLEMENT, Francis Hannah.

DAVIS, Jane (1787–1787)

Jane Davis was the daughter of marine private John Davis and his wife, Martha. The child was born on the *Prince of Wales* on 9 May 1787 just before the First Fleet left Portsmouth and was christened on 4 June. According to both Scott's journal and the Victualling List (T46/22) she died on 12 July 1787.

DEVAN/DIVAN, Edward. See DWAN, Edward.

DOUGHERTY, Daniel (1787–?)

Daniel Dougherty was the son of marine private Arthur Dougherty and his wife, Judith. He was born on the *Prince of Wales* on 10 July 1787 and christened while the fleet was at Rio de Janeiro on 19 August. The family returned to England on the *Gorgon*, leaving the colony on 13 December 1791. Daniel's mother and one of two sisters born in the colony died on this return voyage.

DOWNEY/BELLAMY, Joseph (1788)

Joseph Downey was the son of the seaman Joseph Downey and the convict Sarah Bellamy. Sarah was one of the youngest female convicts on the fleet— both she and fellow-convict Esther Abrahams were about seventeen when they disembarked. The child was born on the *Lady Penrhyn* towards the end of the voyage. He was christened at Port Jackson on 10 February 1788 as Joseph Downey and died two weeks later on 29 February.

DUTTON, Francis Hannah. See CLEMENT, Francis Hannah.

DWAN/DEVAN/DIVAN, Edward (1787–?)

Edward Dwan was the son of a marine sergeant of the same name and his wife, Jane. He was born on the *Charlotte* just before the First Fleet left Portsmouth and was christened on 20 April 1787. He returned to England with his family on the *Gorgon*, leaving the colony on 13 December 1791. His two younger brothers who had been born in Port Jackson both died on this return voyage.

EVANS, Elizabeth. See JONES, ?

FINN, Daniel (1787)

Daniel Finn was possibly the stillborn son of Mary Finn, convict. This birth is only recorded in Surgeon Bowes Smyth's list of children (ML Mss 995). No further record of the child's presence on the Fleet has been found.

FOWLES, Mary (c.1782–?)

Mary Fowles was the daughter of Ann Fowles, convict. The child presumably stayed with her mother in Newgate Prison for about two years before embarkation on the *Lady Penrhyn* on 9 January 1787.

On 17 February 1789, in an act of philanthropic abduction, Captain Phillip took the child from her mother—'a woman of abandoned character' (Collins)—and sent her to Norfolk Island. This act was meant to save the girl from moral contagion. She was sent there together with the three-year-old orphan Edward Parkinson (qv). Both were educated and maintained at public expense. By mid-June 1794 Mary was in service to the assistant surgeon, Thomas Jamison.

GOUGH/COX, Joseph (c.1780–?)

Joseph Gough was the son of a corporal of the marines, Thomas Gough, and his wife, Johanna. The family sailed on the *Prince of Wales*. As Joseph Cox he was transferred from the marine children's list to the marine list on 1 June 1788. The following month he was listed as a drummer. Joseph returned to England with his parents on board the *Gorgon*, leaving Port Jackson on 13 December 1791.

GREEN, William (c.1785–1787)

William Green was the son of Ann Green/Cowley, convict, who took her baby aboard the *Lady Penrhyn* on 9 January 1787. At her trial his mother stated: '...my husband...died suddenly, three months before this child was born' (Gillen, p. 148). The baby survived for only one month and died on 8 February 1787, before the ship reached Portsmouth.

HARMSWORTH, Ann (c.1783–1828)

Ann Harmsworth was the daughter of marine private Thomas Harmsworth and his wife Alice. The child accompanied her parents and older brother Thomas (qv) on the *Friendship*. Later, at Rio de Janeiro on 22 August 1787, the family was transferred to the *Prince of Wales*. A second brother John (qv) was born on the voyage.

Ann's father died (or was buried) at Port Jackson on 30 April 1788 and her widowed mother married Daniel Stanfield. The new family moved to Norfolk Island in October 1791 and returned to Port Jackson in 1795. As Ann Armsworth she married a private in the New South Wales Corps, Samuel

Marsden, on 19 January 1800. The couple lived on Norfolk Island from 1802 until 1810. She may have had as many as six children and died on 30 July 1828.

HARMSWORTH, John (1787–1860)

John Harmsworth was the son of marine private Thomas Harmsworth and his wife Alice. The child was born on the *Prince of Wales* on 1 December 1787 (see Clark & Scott). The boy's father died at Port Jackson on 30 April 1788 and his widowed mother married Daniel Stanfield. The new family moved to Norfolk Island in October 1791 and returned to Port Jackson in 1795.

At the age of seven John Harmsworth enlisted in the New South Wales Corps (on 4 December 1794) and by 1802 was a drummer. He fathered a child (Sarah) to Sarah Wheeler in 1805 and it is believed they went with him to Van Diemen's Land in 1810 when he was transferred to the 73rd Regiment. He left there with his regiment when it was transferred to Ceylon in 1814.

In 1820 he was discharged, returned to Van Diemen's Land and took up farming. He died there on 21 July 1860. At seventy-two (not seventy-three as reported) he was apparently the last survivor of the First Fleet (see Hobart Town *Daily Mercury*, 23 July 1860, p. 2).

HARMSWORTH, Thomas (1784–1788)

Thomas Harmsworth was the first-born son of a marine private of the same name and his wife, Alice. He was born on 6 March 1784 at Warnford, Hampshire. The child accompanied his parents and younger sister Ann Harmsworth (qv) on the *Friendship*. Later, at Rio de Janeiro on 22 August 1787, the family was transferred to the *Prince of Wales*. Thomas Harmsworth died at Port Jackson on 24 February 1788. (Smee, the 1788 Victualling List and Scott all give 24 February, Gillen gives 25th and St Phillip's Register states he was buried on 25th.)

HART, John (1787–?)

John Hart was the son of John Fisher, a seaman on the *Lady Penrhyn*, and Catherine Hart, convict. Catherine was transferred from the *Lady Penrhyn* to the *Prince of Wales* on 29 August 1787 where the child was born on 6 October. (Scott and the 1787 Victualling List, T 46/22, state 6 October; the ship's log gives 7 October and Gillen, mistakenly, gives 7 September.) The child was christened at the Cape of Good Hope on 21 October.

On 4 March 1790 John Hart went to Norfolk Island on the *Sirius* with his mother and baby brother born in the colony. He was one of five children from the First Fleet, born to a convict mother, who was sent to the island on this vessel.

HAYWARD/HAYWOOD/HAWARD, Elizabeth (c.1773–1836)

Elizabeth Hayward was almost certainly the youngest of the women convicts. On 19 December 1786 she was indicted for stealing clothes from the man to whom she was apprenticed and then pawning them. Elizabeth was sentenced at the Old Bailey in January 1787 to seven years transportation (*OBSP*, 1786–87, trial no. 219, 313, 328). She was delivered to the *Lady Penrhyn* on 22 January where Bowes Smyth gave her age as thirteen.

On 9 February 1788 at Port Jackson she was ordered thirty lashes for insolence. On 4 March 1790 she was sent to Norfolk Island and apparently stayed there until 1813. In that time she bore at least four children. The fathers' names remain unknown. She left Norfolk Island in January 1813 as the wife of Joseph Lowe, accompanied by two of her children. She may be the Elizabeth Lowe whose burial was recorded at St John's, Launceston, on 29 October 1836, aged sixty-six.

HOLMES, Henry. See KABLE, Henry.

HUDSON, John (c.1774–?)

John Hudson, a nine-year-old chimneysweep and orphan, first appeared in the Newgate Gaol Register on 20 October 1783. Then, on 29 October he was indicted for breaking, entering and stealing. He was sentenced to seven years' transportation at the Old Bailey on 10 December 1783 (*OBSP* 1783/84, Trial no. 19, 49 & 161). On 22 December 1783 his name first appears on the list of convicts to be transported to America.

John Hudson was sent aboard the *Mercury* from Newgate Prison on 30 March 1784. After the convict uprising on that vessel he was retaken on 13 April and finally arrived at the *Dunkirk* hulk in June, aged ten.

John Hudson was discharged to the *Friendship* on 11 March 1787 as the youngest male convict on the First Fleet. He was sent to Norfolk Island on 4 March 1790 on the *Sirius* (see HMS *Sirius* muster, March–April 1790, Adm. 36/10978). On 15 February 1791 he received fifty lashes for being outside his hut after hours. There does not appear to be any record of his return from the Island and his life thereafter remains a mystery.

HUGHS, Edward. See PARKINSON, Edward.

JONES, ? (1787)

Elizabeth Jones, convict, miscarried on board the *Lady Penrhyn*, according to the Surgeon's log, on 25 May 1787.

JONES, Jane/Jenny (c.1778–1849)

Jane Jones was probably the child of Elizabeth Jones, convict, who was mustered by Major Ross as Elizabeth Jones alias Elizabeth Evans. The child embarked on the *Lady Penrhyn* on 9 January 1787. On 4 March 1790, both mother and daughter were transferred to Norfolk Island on the *Sirius*. Jane was one of five First Fleet children with convict mothers on this vessel.

Jane Jones married Thomas Rose junior at Sydney on 24 May 1800 and bore two children: Thomas (c.1800) and William (1802). The couple parted in 1803 when her husband and his brother returned to England for a visit. After his return, Thomas did not take up residence with his wife and family.

In 1806 Jane was recorded as living with Matthew Conroy and having four sons. By 1825, as Jane Rose, she was listed with James Walsh and a two-year-old child. In 1828 she was recorded as the wife of James Walsh. If she was the Jane Rose who died at Wollongong on 29 September 1849, then she was the longest surviving free female from the First Fleet.

KABLE/CABELL/CABLE/HOLMES, Henry (1785?–1852)

Henry Kable was born in Norwich Castle Gaol to convict parents Susannah Holmes and Henry Cabell, later Kable. The child's plight aroused widespread interest and charitable concern in England when the mother was refused permission to take her baby with her on the hulk. After a much publicised saga Henry Kable jnr was reunited with both parents on the *Dunkirk* hulk on 15 November 1786: '...yesterday afternoon [I] received on board His Majesty's Ship Dunkirk...a male child, said to be the Son of Susannah Holmes...and at the same time Henry Cabel' (HO 42/10, 410, Henry Bradley to Evan Nepean, 16 November 1786).

In late 1788 his father found someone to write back to the child's paternal grandmother in Suffolk. The letter was published in the *London Chronicle* (21–23 July 1789). The father mentions that 'our little boy Harry is a promising little fellow, and goes to school'. Presumably he must have been at least four. Later still, in a petition to the governor in 1822 (AONSW 4/1838) Henry Kable junior gave his own age as thirty-eight which would mean he was born in 1784 or 1785. His actual tombstone claims that he was born on 17 February 1786. Confusingly, the ABGR claims that he was born on 17 December 1786 and christened on 17 December 1788.

Mother and son were transferred from the *Friendship* to the *Charlotte* at the Cape of Good Hope on 28 October 1787. The child's parents were then one of the first five couples to be married at Port Jackson on 10 February 1788. They produced a further ten children.

Their first son was to become the most favoured and prosperous child of any convict from the First Fleet. His father's shipping and commercial interests and his honourable civic life brought considerable wealth and prestige to the family. Henry Kable, junior, never married and he died on 15 May 1852, supposedly aged sixty-six.

LANGLEY/SKIRVING, Henrietta (1787–1828)

Henrietta Langley was the daughter of convict mother Jane Langley. The child was presumably conceived just after the mother was embarked and was born on the *Lady Penrhyn* at the Cape of Good Hope on 21 October 1787. (The ship's log and the Victualling List T 46/22 record 21 October.) Henrietta was christened on 4 November as Henrietta Skirving (see St Phillip's Register) and it is thought that the father may therefore have been Philip Scriven. (There is still some uncertainty and speculation about the child's paternity.)

Mother and daughter were sent to Norfolk Island on 4 March 1790 on the *Sirius*. She was one of five children from the First Fleet, born to convict mothers, who went on this vessel. By June 1794 Jane Langley was recorded with two additional children and said to be married to Thomas Chipp. The family left the island on the *Daedalus* on 27 November 1794.

On 23 March 1807 Henrietta Langley married Edward Fletcher, convict, at Parramatta. She received land grants in that district and bore seven children between 1808–1828(?). She died on 11 August 1828 and was buried on 14 August at St Peter's, Campbelltown.

LAWSON/ROSSON/RAWSON, Mary/John (c.1787–1787)

The child born to Isabella Lawson/Rosson, convict, on 31 May 1787 is listed, confusingly, as male and then later as female in Surgeon Bowes Smyth's journal. The log of the *Lady Penrhyn* lists the child as a girl. Isabella must have been pregnant at embarkation on 26 January 1787. A convict's child, Mary Lawson, is listed as dead on 8 June 1787.

MCCABE/MCCAVE, Charles (1787)

Charles McCabe was the stillborn son of Eleanor McCabe, convict, and an unidentified seaman. The child was delivered on board the *Lady Penrhyn* on 24 November 1787. Bowes Smyth records the surname as McCave. James Scott records the birth of a girl on the same date but on the *Prince of Wales*.

MASON, Thomas (1786–1787)

Thomas Mason was the son of Betty (Elizabeth) Mason, convict. The child was conceived in Gloucester gaol and born around December 1786. Mother and son embarked on the *Friendship* on 17 April 1787—not 10 April as Gillen's entry for the mother states. Thomas Mason died at sea on 29 September 1787 (see Victualling List T46/22).

MITCHELL, Thomas (1787)

Thomas Mason is only recorded in Surgeon Bowes Smyth's List (ML Mss 995). It is likely that he was the stillborn son of Mary Mitchell, convict, delivered on board the *Lady Penrhyn*.

MORTON/MOULTON, Joshua. See BENTLEY, Joshua.

MULLENS, Mary (c.1783–?)

Mary Mullens was the daughter of Hannah Mullens, convict, who was sentenced to death on 26 April 1786 and reprieved to transportation for life on 4 January 1787. For those eight months the child stayed with her mother in a condemned cell in Newgate Prison. On 26 January 1787 mother and daughter boarded the *Lady Penrhyn*. Although Mary Mullens appears in two of the Victualling Lists during the voyage there is no record of this child later in the colony.

MUNDAY, Edward (c.1783–1832)

Edward Munday was the son of marine private John Munday and his wife Ann. The family may have travelled on the *Sirius*. A brother and sister were born in Port Jackson before the family went to Norfolk Island in October 1791. It is not known when Edward Munday returned to Port Jackson but on 25 July 1802 he joined the New South Wales Corps.

In November 1806 Edward was accused of the murder of Thomas Witington while on sentry duty at Parramatta. In the course of this duty he had challenged a man the requisite three times. When this failed to elicit a response he fired and killed the stranger. Munday was judged to be doing his duty and was acquitted (Court of Criminal Jurisdiction, Minutes of Proceedings, AONSW Reel 2651, 5/1149, 334).

In 1810 Munday was transferred to the 73rd Regiment. It appears he went with the regiment to Ceylon in mid-1814. Much later, around 1826, he is believed to have returned and joined his brother, Clarence Munday, in Van Diemen's Land. Edward Munday died there in May 1832, aged forty-eight.

PARFETT/PARFET, James (1787–?)

James Parfett was the son of marine drummer John Parfett and his wife, Sarah. The child was born on the *Prince of Wales* on 1 June 1787 and christened at Teneriffe on 4 June. Two siblings were born in Port Jackson and the family returned to England on the *Gorgon*, leaving the colony on 13 December 1791.

PARKER, Ann. See PUGH, Ann.

PARKINSON/HUGHS, Edward (c.1784–1798)

Edward Parkinson was the son of Jane Parkinson, convict. They arrived at the *Dunkirk* hulk on 1 November 1786 and presented a problem to the super-intendent Henry Bradley: '[she] brought with her a Male child about Nine Months old; the Gaoler who delivered these people assured me that every means except force, were used in vain to prevent the child being brought here, the mother declaring she would destroy herself if seperated [sic] from her Infant. Pray Sir inform me whether this little one is to accompany its mother to Botany Bay or be returned to Lancaster' (HO 42/10, 405, Henry Bradley to Evan Nepean, 1 November 1786).

Mother and son boarded the *Friendship* and were transferred to the *Lady Penrhyn* on 29 October 1787. On 18 November 1787 Edward's mother died at sea, making him the first child orphaned on the First Fleet. In February 1789 Governor Phillip sent him and Mary Fowles (qv) to Norfolk Island to be maintained at public expense. The boy later left the island by the *Chesterfield* on 10 March 1793. Gillen suggests that during his time on the island he may have been befriended by the ship's master William Raven and went with him on this voyage as a servant. The boy was lost overboard on 3 August 1798, just off Rio de Janeiro.

PRIOR, John Matthew (1787–1788)

John Matthew Prior was the son of Catherine Prior/Pryor/Fryer, convict, and, reputedly, the convict John Arscott. The child was born on the *Charlotte* the day after leaving the Cape of Good Hope on 14 November 1787. He was christened John Matthew Prior on 10 February 1788 and died at Port Jackson on 18 March. Four years later—on 8 December 1792—his parents married.

PUGH/PARKER, Ann/Nancy (1786–1788)

Ann Pugh was the daughter of convict parents Edward Pugh and Elizabeth Parker. The child was born in Gloucester gaol in December 1786 and the family embarked on the *Friendship* on 10 April 1787. Mother and child were transferred to the *Charlotte* at the Cape of Good Hope on 28 October. She died at Port Jackson on 30 June 1788, registered as Ann Pugh.

RAWSON, Mary. See LAWSON, Mary.

RICHARDS, Samuel (1787–?)

Samuel Richards was the son of marine private Laurence Richards and his wife Mary. Born on the *Prince of Wales* on 9 October 1787, he was christened on 21 October 1787 (see St Phillip's Register). In January 1800, aged twelve, Samuel

Richards enlisted in the New South Wales Corps and was later joined by his younger brother William. Together with their father, the boys later transferred to the 73rd Regiment on 24 April 1810. When this regiment was transferred to Ceylon in 1814, both brothers left the colony. No later records have been found.

ROSS, Alexander John (c.1779–1800)

Alexander John Ross was the son of Major Robert Ross who went to New South Wales as lieutenant-governor and commander of the garrison. The boy boarded the *Lady Penrhyn* on 3 May 1787. His father's high rank made this child the most elite young voyager of the entire First Fleet. His only peer and companion of similar age was James Campbell (qv). Lieutenant Clark later described Campbell as Ross's 'old play fellow who I believe writes to him' (Clark, p. 291).

After serving as a volunteer without pay, Alexander Ross was promoted to second lieutenant on 8 February 1789. He accompanied his father to Norfolk Island after Major Ross' appointment as lieutenant-governor in 1790. The boy returned to England with his father on the *Gorgon*, leaving the colony on 13 December 1791.

ROSSON, Mary. See LAWSON, Mary.

RUSSELL, Mary (?–?)

Mary Russell was the daughter of marine private John Russell and his wife, Elizabeth. The child travelled on the *Friendship* and a brother Thomas (qv) was born during the voyage. The family returned to England on the *Gorgon*, leaving the colony on 13 December 1791.

RUSSELL, Thomas (1787–?)

Thomas Russell was the son of marine private John Russell and his wife, Elizabeth. The child was born on the *Friendship* on 3 July 1787 and christened at Rio de Janeiro on 12 August (see St Phillip's Register). It was reported that he was born with a webbed hand and was crippled in the right leg. The family returned to England on the *Gorgon*, leaving the colony on 13 December 1791.

SANDLIN, Hugh (c.1785–1787)

Hugh Sandlin was the child of Ann Sandlin alias Lines, convict, and was christened in London on 12 February 1785. Mother and son embarked on the *Lady Penrhyn* on 9 January 1787. Hugh Sandlin died at Portsmouth before the fleet sailed on 24 April 1787.

SCOTT, Elizabeth (1787–?)

Elizabeth Scott was the daughter of marine sergeant James Scott and his wife, Jane. The child was born on the *Prince of Wales* at Rio de Janeiro on 29 August

1787. She was christened on board by the Reverend Samuel Johnston on 3 September (see Scott, p. 14; St Phillip's Register). The family returned to England on the *Gorgon*, leaving the colony on 13 December 1791.

SKIRVING, Henrietta. See LANGLEY, Henrietta.

SMITH, Ann (c.1785–?)

Ann Smith was estimated by the superintendent of the *Dunkirk* hulk to be about twelve months old when received on board with her convict mother of the same name on 8 December 1786. The child had been conceived in Winchester gaol. They embarked on the *Charlotte* on 12 March 1787. A brother by convict father Patrick Burn was later born in the colony.

The (unmarried) mother and her two children went to Norfolk Island on 4 March 1790 on the *Sirius*. Ann Smith junior was one of five children from the First Fleet, born to convict mothers, who went on this vessel. Mother and daughter returned to Port Jackson in 1793. In 1796, at eleven years of age, Ann Smith was allegedly raped by the free settler Andrew Hume.

SMITH, Edward/William (1786?–1788?)

Edward Smith was listed by Surgeon Bowes Smyth on the *Lady Penrhyn*, aged eleven—this was possibly meant to be eleven months. The child was conceived in Winchester gaol by Hannah Smith, convict. Mother and son were sent to the *Dunkirk* on 7 December 1786. From there they were sent to the *Charlotte*, on 11 March 1787. During the voyage of the First Fleet mother and son were twice more transferred: first to the *Friendship* on 11 August 1787 and then to the *Lady Penrhyn* on 29 October at the Cape of Good Hope. Edward Smith died and was buried at Port Jackson on 6 June 1788.

SPENCE/BRAUND/BRYANT, Charlotte (1787–1792)

Charlotte Spence was the daughter of Mary Braund/Brand/Broad, convict, and was conceived on the *Dunkirk* to an unknown father. The child was born on the *Charlotte* on 8 September 1787 (see Victualling List T 46/22), just after the ship had left Rio de Janeiro. She was christened at the Cape of Good Hope on 28 October as Charlotte Spence—possibly a clue to the father's surname.

Her mother and William Bryant (convict) were married at Port Jackson on 10 February 1788. On 28 March 1791 they escaped in a small fishing boat taking Charlotte, her baby brother Emanuel and seven male convicts with them. Their epic voyage ended ten weeks later in Batavia where Bryant and Charlotte's brother both died. The child and her mother were then embarked on the *Gorgon* which was en route from Port Jackson to England. Charlotte died at sea on 6 May 1792.

SPENCER/SPENCE, Mary (1787–1788)

Mary Spencer was the daughter of a convict mother of the same name. The child was born on the *Prince of Wales* on 1 July 1787 (see Victualling List T 46/22) and christened on 19 August (see St Phillip's Register). Mother and daughter were disembarked on 6 February 1788 and the child died at Port Jackson on 5 April 1788.

STEWART, John (?–?)

John Stewart was one of two sons of marine sergeant Peter Stewart and his wife, Margaret, who sailed on the *Friendship*. John and his brother Robert (qv) and their parents returned to England on the *Gorgon*, leaving the colony on 13 December 1791.

STEWART, Robert (?–?)

Robert Stewart was one of two sons of marine sergeant Peter Stewart and his wife, Margaret, who sailed on the *Friendship*. He was described by Lieutenant Clark as 'a Sweet little fellow'. On 18 July 1787 Robert was almost killed when one of the male convicts accidentally dropped him into the forehold. Robert and his brother John (qv) and their parents returned to England on the *Gorgon*, leaving the colony on 13 December 1791.

THEAKSTON/YEATS, Joseph (c.1787–?)

Joseph Theakston vies with James Baughan (qv) as the most elusive child of the First Fleet. Joseph is recorded by Surgeon Bowes Smyth as born on the voyage although his name does not appear in any of the Victualling Lists. It is believed that Joseph was the son of Nancy Yeats, convict, and a sailor, Joseph Theakston, both of whom travelled on the *Lady Penrhyn*. A child was christened Joseph Theakston at Port Jackson on 16 March 1788 (see St Phillip's Register).

THOMAS, James (1787?–1788)

James Thomas was the son of marine private Samuel Thomas and his wife, Ann. His parents embarked on the *Sirius* and later transferred to the *Alexander*. The child was presumably born on the voyage and was christened on 3 February 1788 (see St Phillip's Register). James Thomas died on 13 April 1788 at Port Jackson.

TILLEY, William. See ABEL, William.

WRIGHT, Elizabeth (1787–?)

Elizabeth Wright was the daughter of marine private Matthew Wright and his wife, Mary. The child was born on the *Prince of Wales* on 17 October 1787 (see Scott and the 1787 Victualling List T 46/22) and christened at the Cape of Good Hope on 21 October (see St Phillip's Register). A sister was born in Port Jackson. The family returned to England on the *Gorgon*, leaving the colony on 13 December 1791.

WRIGHT/CHARLICUT, Mary Ann (1787?–?)

Mary Ann Wright was the daughter of marine private Henry Wright and his wife, Ann. The child embarked with her parents on the *Prince of Wales*. Mary Ann may have been born just prior to departure for she was not christened until 19 August 1787 when the ship reached Rio de Janeiro. This christening is inexplicably recorded in the St Phillip's Register under the name 'Charlicut'.

Once in the colony, Mary Ann's father was convicted of raping a young girl, Elizabeth Chapman (qv), the daughter of a fellow marine. Mary Ann and her mother separated from the father and returned to England on the *Gorgon*, leaving the colony on 13 December 1791.

YEATS, Joseph. See THEAKSTON, Joseph.

YOUNG, John (?–?)

John Young was one of two sons of the marine sergeant Thomas Young and his wife, Elizabeth. The child accompanied his parents and brother Thomas (qv) on the *Friendship*. The family returned to England on the *Gorgon*, leaving the colony on 13 December 1791.

YOUNG, Thomas (?–?)

Thomas Young was one of two sons, presumably the elder, of marine sergeant Thomas Young and his wife, Elizabeth. The child accompanied his parents and brother John (qv) on the *Friendship*. The family returned to England on the *Gorgon*, leaving the colony on 13 December 1791.

YOUNGSON, George (c. 1774–?)

George Youngson was twelve when he was arrested, together with his older sister Elizabeth, on 16 September 1786. They were charged with house-breaking and the theft of money (PRO P1 27/6). He was sentenced to death on 26 March 1787. On 16 April the sentence was amended to seven years' transportation (PRO Palatinate of Lancaster Rolls 1787, 25/177).

George Youngson was sent to the *Prince of Wales* together with Elizabeth on 13 May 1787—the very day the First Fleet departed. George was sent to Norfolk Island in February 1789 and returned from there in November 1794. His life thereafter is unknown.

CHECKLIST OF CHILDREN

Born on the First Fleet before embarkation

Abel, William
Davis, Jane
Dwan, Edward

Died on the First Fleet before embarkation

Green, William
Sandlin, Hugh

Embarked on the First Fleet

Abel, William
Abrahams, Esther
Bagley, Maria
Bolton, Rebecca
Campbell, James
Chapman, Elizabeth
Chapman, Jane
Colethread, James
Davis, Jane
Dwan, Edward
Fowles, Mary
Gough, Joseph
Harmsworth, Ann
Harmsworth, Thomas
Hayward, Elizabeth
Hudson, John
Jones, Jane

Kable, Henry
Mason, Thomas
Mullens, Mary
Munday, Edward
Parkinson, Edward
Pugh, Ann
Ross, Alexander
Russell, Mary
Smith, Ann
Smith, Edward
Stewart, John
Stewart, Robert
Wright, Mary Ann
Young, John
Young, Thomas
Youngson, George

Born on the First Fleet during the voyage

Bacon, Elizabeth
Baughan, James
Bentley, Joshua
Clement, Francis Hannah
Dougherty, Daniel
Downey, Joseph
Harmsworth, John
Hart, John
Langley, Henrietta
Lawson, Mary
Parfett, James
Prior, John
Richards, Samuel
Russell, Thomas
Scott, Elizabeth
Spence, Charlotte
Spencer, Mary
Theakston, Joseph
Thomas, James
Wright, Elizabeth

Died on the First Fleet during the voyage

Davis, Jane
Lawson, Mary
Mason, Thomas

Miscarriages and stillbirths on the First Fleet during the voyage

Colley, William
Collpitts, John
Finn, Daniel
Jones, ?
McCabe, Charles
Mitchell, Thomas

SELECT BIBLIOGRAPHY

(a) Seventeenth, Eighteenth and Nineteenth Century Sources

'An Account of the Nature and Views of the Philanthropic Society...for the Prevention of Crimes, by the Admission of the Offspring of Convicts, and for the Reform of the Criminal Poor Children', Philanthropic Society, London, 1797.

'An Account of the Nature and Views of the Philanthropic Society...for the Prevention of Crimes, by the Admission of the Offspring of Convicts, and for the Reform of the Criminal Poor Children', Philanthropic Society London, 1799.

Andrews, James Pettit, *An Appeal to the Humane, on behalf of the Most Deplorable Class of Society, The Climbing Boys, Employed by the Chimney-Sweepers*, John Stockdale, London, 1788.

Armstrong, George, *An Account of the Diseases Most Incident to Children*, T. Caddell, London, 1783.

British Parliamentary Papers: Correspondence and Papers relating to Convict Ships, Convict Discipline and Transportation, 1843–47, Irish University Press, Shannon, reprint, 1969, vol. 7. See particularly pp. 521–61 on homosexuality in convict society.

Buchan, William, *Domestic Medicine*, H. Chamberlaine et al., Dublin, 1784.

Cadogan, William, *An Essay upon Nursing, and the Management of Children, from their Birth to Three Years of Age*, J. Roberts, London, 1748.

Clark, Ralph, *The Journal and Letters of Lt. Ralph Clark, 1787–1792*, Paul G. Fidlon (ed.), Australian Documents Library, Sydney, 1981.

Collins, David, *An Account of the English Colony in New South Wales*, A. H. & A. W. Reed, Sydney, 1975.

Denman, Thomas, *Introduction to the Practice of Midwifery*, (self-published), London, 1782.

Dornford, Josiah, *Nine Letters to the Right Honourable the Lord Mayor and Aldermen of the City of London, on the State of the City Prisons*, (self-published), London, 1786.

Hanway, Jonas, *The Neglect of the Effectual Separation of Prisoners, and the Want of Good Order and Religious Oeconomy in Our Prisons*, (self-published), London, 1784.

Hanway, Jonas, *Observations on the Causes of the Dissoluteness which Reigns among the Lower Classes of the People...Likewise a Plan for Preventing the Extraordinary Mortality of the Children of the Labouring Poor in London and Westminster*, Marine Society, London, 1772.

Hanway, Jonas, *A Sentimental History of Chimney-sweepers*, Dodsley, London, 1785.

Howard, John, *The State of the Prisons in England and Wales*, William Eyres, Warrington, 1777 (1st edn).

Howard, John, *The State of the Prisons in England and Wales*, William Eyres, Warrington, 1784 (3rd edn).

Hunter, John, *An Historical Journal of Transactions at Port Jackson and Norfolk Island*, Libraries Board of South Australia, Adelaide, 1968.

Journals of the House of Commons, November the 15th, 1787, to September the 25th, 1788, vol. 43, House of Commons, London, 1803.

King, Philip Gidley, *The Journal of Philip Gidley King; Lieutenant, R. N. 1787–1790*, Paul G. Fidlon (ed.), Australian Documents Library, Sydney, 1980.

Montgomery, James (ed.) *The Chimney-Sweeper's Friend, and Climbing-Boy's Album*, Longman et al., London, 1824.

Moss, William, *An Essay on the Management and Nursing of Children in the Earlier Periods of Infancy*, J. Johnson, London, 1781.

Nelson, James, *An Essay on the Government of Children*, R. & J. Dodsley, London, 1753.

Phillip, Arthur, *The Voyage of Governor Phillip to Botany Bay*, Libraries Board of South Australia, Adelaide, 1968.

'Report of the Committee of the Society for the Improvement of Prison Discipline, and for the Reformation of Juvenile Offenders', The Society, London, 1818.

'Report of the Committee of the Society for the Improvement of Prison Discipline, and for the Reformation of Juvenile Offenders', The Society, London, 1820.

Smyth, Arthur Bowes, *The Journal of Arthur Bowes Smyth: Surgeon, Lady Penrhyn, 1787–1789*, Australian Documents Library, Sydney, 1979.

Tench, Watkin, *Sydney's First Four Years: Being a Reprint of A Narrative of the Expedition to Botany Bay*, Angus & Robertson, Sydney, 1961.

W., 'Sweep, Soot O! or, Some Account of Little Jem, the Chimney-sweeper and his Benefactress,' J. Marshall, London, [c.1797].

White, John, *Journal of a Voyage to New South Wales*, Angus & Robertson, Sydney, 1962.

Worgan, George, *Journal of a First Fleet Surgeon*, Library Council of NSW, Sydney, 1978.

Zouch, H., *Hints respecting the Public Police*, John Stockdale, London, 1786.

(b) Modern Sources

Bouce, Paul-Gabriel (ed.), *Sexuality in Eighteenth Century Britain*, Manchester University Press, Manchester, 1982.

Carpenter, Kenneth, *Improving the Lot of the Chimney Sweeps*, Arno Press, New York, 1972.

Cunningham, Hugh, *The Children of the Poor: Representations of Childhood since the Seventeenth Century*, Blackwell, Oxford, 1991.

de Mause, Lloyd (ed.), *The History of Childhood: The Evolution of Parent-child Relationships as a Factor in History*, Souvenir Press, London, 1980.

Dobash, Russell, *The Imprisonment of Women*, Blackwell, Oxford, 1986.

Ekirch, Roger, *Bound for America: The Transportation of British Convicts to the Colonies, 1718–1775*, Clarendon Press, Oxford, 1987.

Emsley, Clive, *Crime and Society in England, 1750–1900*, Longman, London, 1987.

Fildes, Valerie (ed.), *Women as Mothers in Pre-Industrial England*, Routledge, London, 1990.

Frost, Alan, *Botany Bay Mirages: Illusions of Australia's Convict Beginnings*, Melbourne University Press, Melbourne, 1994.

George, Dorothy, *London Life in the Eighteenth Century*, Penguin, London, 1992.

Gillen, Mollie, *The Founders of Australia: A Biographical Dictionary of the First Fleet*, appendices by Yvonne Browning & Michael Flynn, Library of Australian History, Sydney, 1989.

Jarrett, Derek, *England in the Age of Hogarth*, Yale University Press, New Haven & London, 1974.

McLynn, Frank, *Crime and Punishment in Eighteenth-Century England*, Routledge, London, 1989.

Phillips, George, *England's Climbing-Boys: A History of the Long Struggle to Abolish Child Labor in Chimneysweeping*, Harvard University Graduate School of Business Administration, Boston, 1949.

Pollock, Linda, *Forgotten Children: Parent–Child Relations from 1500 to 1900*, Cambridge University Press, Cambridge, 1988.

Porter, Roy, *English Society in the Eighteenth Century*, Penguin, London, 1990.

Robinson, Portia, *The Hatch and Brood of Time: A Study of the First Generation of Native-born White Australians 1788–1828*, Oxford University Press, Melbourne, 1985.

Rousseau, G. S. & Roy Porter (eds), *Sexual Underworlds of the Enlightenment*, Manchester University Press, Manchester, 1987.

Stone, Lawrence, *The Family, Sex and Marriage in England 1500–1800*, Weidenfeld & Nicolson, London, 1977.

Strange, Katherine, *Climbing Boys: A Study of Sweeps' Apprentices 1773–1875*, Allison & Busby, London, 1982.

Styles, John, 'Sir John Fielding and the Problem of Criminal Investigation in Eighteenth-Century England,' *Transactions of the Royal Historical Society*, fifth series no. 33, 1983, pp. 127–149.

Taylor, James Stephen, *Jonas Hanway: Founder of the Marine Society*, Scolar Press, London & Berkeley, 1985.

Wilson, Adrian, *The Making of Man—Midwifery: Childbirth in England 1660–1770*, UCL Press, London, 1995.

LIFE AND ADVENTURES: 1776–1801
John Nicol
Edited and introduced by Tim Flannery

'A rare treat...Nicol was a cooper by trade and sailed in a great
variety of vessels and capacities. He twice circumnavigated the
globe, saw action in the American War of Independence and
sailed to Port Jackson aboard a convict transport...The result
is a charming account of the world seen through the eyes of a
kindly and thoughtful man with a great capacity for empathy, a
tremendous eye for detail and, apparently, a spectacular
memory.' *Sunday Age*

'This remarkable little book defies the normal course of
historical writing and gives us a uniquely personal view of the
world as seen from the focsle in the late 18th century...
Tim Flannery is to be congratulated for having the eye to
breathe life back into a person whose story engages readers
today as much as when it was first written.'
Sydney Morning Herald

'It's a knockout...Nicol is a sunny, charming, highly observant
guide and a first-rate storyteller.'
Sun-Herald

'Spectacularly observant...ranks with many of the better
known classics.'
Age

208pp, paperback, rrp $19.70, ISBN 1 875847 41 3